OICE   ABO   RI
PINESS   ABOU   T
R FORMULA   ABO
TRENGTH   ABOUT
ONS   ABOUT YOU
TIVATION   ABOUT
UT THE ELEMENTS
T RELATIONSHIPS
BOUT THE PLAN

HE END   ABOUT CH

R LIFE   ABOUT HAP

RNEY   ABOUT YOU

ASSION   ABOUT ST

ACY   ABOUT SEAS

NTRA   ABOUT AC

FORMANCE   ABOU

UT WORK   ABOU

BOUT BALANCE   A

PRAISE FOR *THIS IS THE THING*

"Are you trying to figure out the purpose of your life? Shane Jackson's book will show you the essence of personal purpose . . . that serving others and choosing joy in our circumstances are two of the game changers that bring meaning to life. Don't miss this instruction manual for living your best life."

—CHERYL BACHELDER, lead director, Chick-fil-A, Inc.; former CEO, Popeyes, Louisiana Kitchen, Inc.; and author, *Dare to Serve*

"Purpose is within your reach—that's the message Shane Jackson conveys in this book that is refreshingly actionable and full of inspiration. I defy you to leave this book without a plan for how you will start to truly 'own' your purpose. Shane delivers wisdom that we can readily implement into our lives and can help you live authentically in your purpose. Must-read!"

—ALEX WEBER, American Ninja Warrior, international keynote speaker, and award-winning entertainer

"*This Is the Thing* is an inspirational road map for intentionally recognizing and acting upon what you want your life to be. Shane's wisdom and advice will leave you full of aspiration with approachable ideas for realizing your personal and timeless intentions."

—TOM PRICE, MD, 23rd US Secretary of Health and Human Services

"*This Is the Thing* is an inspiring, motivating, and practical road map to achieve and experience joy, fulfillment, and purpose in life. For me, it was an inspiring, entertaining, and fulfilling reading experience. It is the best book on how to create and incorporate healthy life principles for responsible stewardship I have ever read. An investment in this book will yield priceless returns. It will change your life for the better!"

—ROSS MASON, founder of HINRI (The High Impact Network of Responsible Innovators)

"Through engaging anecdotes and relatable lessons, *This Is the Thing* makes the central question of finding life's purpose feel accessible and achievable. Shane Jackson provides wisdom in finding the 'symbiosis in life' of work, relationships, and self that leads to experiencing a joyful life."

—JACK HARRIS, CEO, Junior Achievement USA; president and CEO, 3DE Schools

"The perfect message for anyone who has reached the pinnacle of their pursuit of a career, life goals, or whatever they thought was important, only to feel empty at the end. Shane Jackson captures the essence of this realization—why you feel this way and how you refocus on what is truly important. A true gift for any young adult trying to figure out what success and happiness truly mean."

—**ANDREW WEXLER,** CEO, Herschend Enterprises

"Early in my career as a pastor, I made a startling discovery. People aren't on a truth quest. They're on a happiness quest. As someone who made their living dispensing truth, well, it was a bit disconcerting. We're all tempted to pursue happiness as if it were a destination. Turns out, it's not. Happiness is a result. A result of what? Thanks to my friend Shane Jackson and his wonderful book This Is the Thing, you're about to find out."

—**ANDY STANLEY,** best-selling author; host, *Your Move with Andy Stanley*; and pastor, North Point Ministries

"Life is a journey of choices and self-discovery, where each chapter we write defines our legacy. Shane Jackson reminds us in his new book to embrace this journey we are on with passion, strength, and balance. This book provides simple, yet profound questions, insights, and examples that allow the reader to reflect on their values, examine their passions, and align their actions with their beliefs to help uncover the masterpiece of who they truly are."

—**RYAN NECE,** former NFL player; managing partner, Next Legacy Partners

"*This Is the Thing* will challenge you, fill you with a desire to aspire to new heights, and create a new paradigm for what is ahead on your leadership journey. If you follow Shane's advice to be really intentional about your life and to act on that intention with his very approachable ideas, you will find great joy and meaning in your life."

—**RICK LYTLE,** PhD, president and CEO, CEO Forum

"If you're a successful business leader who is thinking, *there's got to be more to life than this*, you're probably right. And Shane Jackson's This Is the Thing is a great guide to help you figure it out."

—**TIM SPIKER,** leadership advisor; author, *The Only Leaders Worth* Following*; and host, *Be Worth* Following* podcast

"*This Is the Thing* is a generous book with the power to move you closer toward your purpose, regardless of your age or stage in life. Everyone needs to read this."

—**JEB BUSH,** 43rd governor of Florida and founder and chairman of ExcelinEd

"Shane Jackson has written a powerful book that addresses the most profound questions in our lives in a clear, approachable way. Who should read this book? Anyone who sees value in taking the time to think about and improve the purpose and direction of their life."

—**FRANK BLAKE,** former CEO of The Home Depot

"Regardless of what season of life you may find yourself in, Shane Jackson's latest book is an existential masterclass on reflection, recalibration, and renewal. Full of personal stories, challenging exercises, and practical next steps, I highly recommend this book for anyone who is not only seeking to fulfill his or her purpose but also striving to become a better human."

—**BRANDON SMITH,** "The Workplace Therapist," cofounder and president, The Worksmiths

"I love Shane Jackson. Shane loves his team, and his team loves their customers! That's a remarkable culture that flows out of the joy, passion, and purpose of the individual. Read this book and you will be inspired and challenged. "

—**CHRIS CARNEAL,** founder, owner, and CEO, Booster

"Shane Jackson's new book is much like sitting around a roaring fire pit with a best friend contemplating the pillars of life. Jackson masterfully weaves together empathy and truth, stripping away life's shallow platitudes and laying bare the fundamental choices we all encounter in experiencing a life well lived. While leading the reader on a journey of discovery of individual purpose and passion, he empowers us all to stand in that purpose with humility, joy, and gratitude. This book is a must-read for everyone seeking a life worthwhile."

—**HEATHER ROBERTSON FORTNER,** MS, IACCP, chair and CEO, SignatureFD

"Ultimately, this book explores the search for meaning in our lives, often referred to as 'happiness.' Shane Jackson helps us recognize that happiness is far more profound and multifaceted than our conventional understanding of it. The process Shane outlines guides us on a soul-searching journey to uncover what truly matters to each of us—our values and beliefs. This book shows us how to embody these values in a way that leads to genuine happiness and meaning in life."

—**MARY BURNS,** MD; psychiatrist, Skyland Trail; clinical assistant professor of psychiatry, Emory University

THIS
IS THE
THING

*About Life, Joy, and
Owning Your Purpose*

SHANE JACKSON

GREENLEAF
BOOK GROUP PRESS

This book is intended as a reference volume only. It is sold with the understanding that the publisher and author are not engaged in rendering any professional services. The material presented is for informational purposes and intended for self-discovery and to broaden your horizons, but is not intended for treatment. If you suspect that you have a problem that might require professional treatment or advice, you should seek competent help.

Published by Greenleaf Book Group Press
Austin, Texas
www.gbgpress.com

Copyright © 2025 Shane Jackson

Thank you to Travis Dommert at Quadrant 2 for the insight and incredible conversations over the years about stress and recovery in developing images 13.1 and 13.2 in this book. Travis was influenced by another great thinker, Jim Blair at the Human Performance Institute.

Distributed by Greenleaf Book Group

For ordering information or special discounts for bulk purchases, please contact Greenleaf Book Group at PO Box 91869, Austin, TX 78709, 512.891.6100.

Design and composition by Greenleaf Book Group and Sheil Parr
Cover design by Greenleaf Book Group and Jonathan Lewis

Publisher's Cataloging-in-Publication data is available.

Print ISBN: 979-8-88645-287-7

eBook ISBN: 979-8-88645-288-4

To offset the number of trees consumed in the printing of our books, Greenleaf donates a portion of the proceeds from each printing to the Arbor Day Foundation. Greenleaf Book Group has replaced over 50,000 trees since 2007.

Printed in the United States of America on acid-free paper

25 26 27 28 29 30 31 32   10 9 8 7 6 5 4 3 2 1

First Edition

This book is dedicated to Jesse and Gertrude Jones, Henry and Mary Price, Vicki Justus, Wiley and Ercyle Walker, and Dale and Lorene Crow—grandparents to me and my wife. The legacy of their lives has rippled through time to touch us and, now, our children. I am forever grateful.

Contents

Introduction

OFTEN THE QUESTIONS WE ask aren't the ones we really want to ask. Maybe it's from a fear of being inappropriate or rude by bringing up things that aren't normally spoken of. Or maybe embarrassment that we are still trying to figure something out that surely everyone else has already figured out. Or maybe because we just can't muster the energy to say what we really want to say.

But more often, rather than being afraid to ask the real questions, we're afraid to give the real answers.

At least, I am.

Over the past few years I have received more and more invitations to speak to audiences around the country as business leaders and particularly people in the healthcare industry want my viewpoint. Organizers almost always ask me to talk about content from my first book or the lessons I have learned in business and leadership that may be beneficial to their audience.

I usually take questions at the end of my speeches. These Q&A sessions generally follow a similar pattern: The questions start slowly as people try to think of something smart to say and then pick up a little as the conversation progresses. From my viewpoint at the podium, I can always tell who in the audience thinks it's an interesting question by whether they are looking at me or looking down at their phone.

But occasionally, something different happens. Someone will ask a question that has nothing to do with business. The attention and energy in the room sharpens and everyone looks up intently. It's as if they are thinking, "I can't believe they just asked that, but I really want to hear how he answers this." The question is disguised as being a personal one about me, but everyone knows it's really about the questioner. Just by asking the question they are disclosing to everyone in the room that they are asking something about my life because they feel unhealthy, unbalanced, and unhappy in theirs.

But I am the one who has been put on the spot.

A few years ago, I was in a private discussion with one of our company's most senior leaders. She asked me a question that got my attention: "How do you do it?"

"How do I do what?"

"How do you do all of it? How do you run this company, have a family, stay in shape, have a life? How do you stay present with so many distractions? And how do you not get down when there are so many hard things going on?"

Personal questions feel risky because the answers cause exposure. If the questioner doesn't like the answer, they may judge you. Or worse, once they understand your convictions they may feel judged by you.

Our natural defensive response to risk causes us to shy away from giving the real answers that expose us. My go-to in these kinds of moments was to demur with platitudes and surface-level answers that, while true, generally leave the questioner placated but unsatisfied. "It's not all that it seems," or "I've got great people around me," or "I guess I'm good at time management." I began to give one of those types of answers and then paused.

Maybe it was the way she asked, the strain I could hear in her voice, or the desperation in her eyes as she was obviously struggling under the many demands of her life. Maybe it was guilt over not giving an honest answer to the previous ten people who had asked me something personal. For whatever reason, that day I tentatively began to share some of my most deeply held beliefs with her. Once I started, the dam opened. Suddenly I looked at the clock and realized I had been speaking for almost forty-five minutes.

"Sorry, I didn't mean to preach at you for so long," I said.

She responded, "No! I have never heard those ideas expressed that way. That is really powerful!"

At my next speech after that encounter, I entered the Q&A session with the recurring fear of getting a question that I wouldn't want to answer. Sure enough, someone took the microphone and asked me something that, if I was going to answer honestly, would require me to disclose something deeply personal. I confess I don't remember the question, but I do remember the awkward silence that followed as I stood on stage contemplating whether and how to answer. Finally, I let go of my fear.

In front of hundreds of people, I opened up about my journey. I confessed the struggles I have had of making sense of life, the many places I have gone searching for wisdom, and finally the simple yet profound answers I have discovered. And most importantly the incredible peace and joy I have found through the process.

Amazingly, after the speech, no one in the line of people waiting to talk to me brought up anything about my presentation—they all wanted to talk about their own lives. Their reactions, and the hundreds of similar ones I have received in the years since, have revealed how common our yearning to get something more out of life is. While we rarely talk about it, we are all struggling not only to make sense of it all, but also, more importantly, to actually do something that breaks us away from our feelings of pain, frustration, or isolation and into an experience that is, well, just better.

All of these interactions are with people who are visibly success-ful on the outside but obviously craving more on the inside. They have helped me realize the danger of not asking real questions and giving honest answers. And giving real answers to others has forced me to give real answers to myself. If we don't ask the real questions, we'll never get the answers we crave, but if we don't give the real answers, we'll never get the change we need.

I don't know what caused you to pick up this book.

Maybe you've never thought about the purpose of your life. You are doing well, having fun, and enjoying what life has to offer. You work hard, but things seem to come easily, and you just assume that everything will work out. If this describes you—congratulations! You are enjoying a pretty rare kind and time of life. Maybe you are reading this book begrudgingly—only satisfying the recommendation of a friend, parent, or boss. Or maybe, just maybe, it's because deep inside, you suspect that, while you seem to generally enjoy life, there has to be something more. That you are missing out.

Perhaps you consider yourself to be someone who is rather self-aware and continually seeks more in life. You read the books and listen to the podcasts of all the latest gurus. Maybe you consider yourself a person of faith and search for truth in ancient teachings. But you get frustrated with all the self-help guides. Which are you supposed to do? Wait, how many different parts of me are there? How much should I exercise? Am I supposed to eat carbs now or has that changed?

Most likely, you are in the group of us who are just surviving. You work hard to make ends meet, but it feels like you can never quite catch up after the latest surprise expense. You try to be a good friend, spouse, or parent, but it feels like you are always letting someone down or they have let you down. You know you should take care of yourself better, and last year you even joined a gym, but after a month the reality of life set in, and you stopped going.

Most of the time you are merely going through the motions of the routines of your life. You feel like you are always just trying to keep all the plates spinning. You have some fun—occasionally go on a vacation, go out with friends, or do some hobby that you enjoy. But once that is over, it only makes going back to your routine even worse. When you do get to occasionally pause, you ask yourself things like:

"Is this all there is?"

"Does anything I do matter?"

"What's the point?"

And when you are honest, you admit to yourself that this isn't what you thought your life would be like. The optimistic young you would look at who you are today and be disappointed. You were going to be different. You were going to make a difference. You were going to run the business, run a marathon, and see the world. What happened?

Or maybe you actually did all those things. You earned the fortune, bought the house, saw the sites, and achieved the goals you set for yourself. But the morning after the party, the day after the race, or the second time you drove the new car, you wondered:

"Why do I still feel empty?"

Perhaps there was a time when you were happy. You remember the happy times, the optimistic times. You remember having friends, having fun, and laughing. But then tragedy struck, and nothing has ever been the same. And the question you keep asking is:

"Why did this happen to me?"

Time and time again I have heard people express these kinds of desperate emotions. Our stories are different, but the storyline is the same: We long for something—something different from this. We want to feel fulfilled—to feel at least one moment of fulfillment. We want to find some meaning to it all.

The words we often actually say are: "I just need to figure out what will make me happy."

If you've ever felt this way, then you're not alone. And there's good news: I believe there are answers.

In the pages ahead, we are going to dive into the hard questions. We will gain perspective through exploring subjects that are often avoided and taking time to understand the amazingly simple and beautiful answers that shape how we view our life. But we won't leave these answers in the realm of philosophical theory. After some honest reflection and self-examination, we will consider every part of our life so that we can apply our answers in ways that help us experience a different kind of life today and start our journey toward more purposeful living.

Now I want to be clear, very few of the ideas behind what I have written about in this book are original to me. One of the most fortunate parts of my life is that I have been exposed to so many incredibly wise people. Over the years, I have synthesized the lessons I've learned from them into a philosophy that has guided how I think about my life and, most importantly, how I make decisions. What I hope is that by putting many of those lessons together, you will discover something that will enable you to start living in an entirely new way.

No matter where you are in life, no matter what questions you are asking, and no matter how you are struggling, I believe there is a way for you to experience the best of what life has to offer.

But here is a warning: Discovering honest answers to real questions is hard work. And frankly, you won't ever find them all, and the ones you do find will change over time. This isn't a one and done. It's step after step along a difficult, challenging, up and down journey.

But what a wonderful journey it can be.

Now let's get started.

PART 1:

PERSPECTIVE

"But the Hebrew word, the word *timshel*—'Thou mayest'—that gives a choice. It might be the most important word in the world. That says the way is open. That throws it right back on a man. For if 'Thou mayest'—it is also true that 'Thou mayest not.'"

—John Steinbeck, *East of Eden*

CHAPTER 1

About the End

TO UNDERSTAND YOUR LIFE, and the purpose of it, you must understand what happens when your life is over.

Wait. Death? (I warned you this journey would be uncomfortable!)

No one likes to think about, much less talk about, death. We try to stay away from funerals because they are all about death. Funerals are, well, sad. And most of what we do in life is to help us avoid sadness. Some funerals remind us of past times that seemed happier and point out the bleakness of our current situation. Other funerals remind us of terrible times that we have worked hard to forget.

Funerals are but one of many rituals that humans have created. While our society in general has become much more casual, we still adhere to some sort of ritual to mark significant events and important moments. We don a cap and gown and walk across a stage to mark the end of formal education. We stand in front of friends and exchange rings to signify the beginning of a marriage.

We blow out candles as people sing a silly song on our birthday. We pray before meals. We tuck our kids in before they go to sleep.

Each of these rituals is meant to make us pause and consider something important—an achievement, a person, or an event. Rituals often benefit both the person participating and those observing. Weddings make the couple stop and consider their vows to each other as they state them publicly, while also reminding those in attendance of the commitments they have made or long to make. A birthday party makes the guest of honor feel appreciated and causes the guests to consider how important that person is as a part of their lives.

We go through rituals because our nature tends to rush us past things without pausing to recognize something worth recognizing. The ritual forces us to focus on things we might otherwise miss. Ceremonies are more than just symbolic; they create moments to think and make unconscious things conscious.

But what about funerals, and specifically: What about our own funeral? It's certainly not a moment to think, because we're not exactly there—we're dead. Why do we have funerals? Why does every culture have some traditional ritual involving the deceased?

Because a funeral isn't for the dead. A funeral is only for the living.

There is something in us that needs to contemplate death because it gives us perspective on our life. We don't enjoy this, but we know it's true. Funerals make us feel emotions that cause us to want to change what we do while we are alive. We have all left a funeral and said things like:

"I need to take better care of myself."

"I need to do something more with my life."

"I need to call my mom more often."

We have also probably left a funeral asking ourselves questions, such as:

"What will people say about me when I'm gone?"

What is it about death that makes us reexamine our life? Why does the end of someone else's life cause us to want to change ours? Is it the inevitable change in our routines that will occur now that the other person is no longer here? Often that is true. But why do I become suddenly contemplative upon hearing of the death of someone I didn't personally know? The death of others reminds us that we too will die. That someday it will be my body in the box. That people will gather to mourn me. Or worse: they won't.

Thinking about my death forces me to ask uncomfortable questions about how I am living my life. My view of death, what it means and what I believe happens after it, ultimately determines what I do in life.

What really happens after I die?

All of us are working toward something. We have to work because we must acquire the things we need to survive, but for many people (and if you are reading this you are most likely in this category), we are working because we want to consume much more than we actually need.

I have a lot of clothes. Certainly, a lot more than I need. I have several different pairs of shoes, shirts, sweaters, jackets. I really like baseball caps and have a whole shelf full of them. It's kind of fun to pick out which cap I'm going to wear. I know I don't need all those things in my closet. I mean, I can only wear one thing at a time, so my clothes spend most of the time just hanging in the closet being used or seen by no one. I could wear the same thing to work every day (assuming I did laundry every night), but I have all this stuff anyway.

When I'm gone, all those clothes will be thrown away, along with most everything else I have collected. No one is going to want all my junk. Even my awesome record collection will eventually end up in a landfill.

So if I don't need all this stuff, why do I have it?

We get pleasure from consumption. We enjoy the food, the drink, the intrigue, the thrill. And here is something we all know but don't like to talk about—the pleasure we get from these things diminishes over time. To get the same level of pleasure, we must consume more. What used to be exciting is now, well, less exciting. Or maybe even boring. We continually need more, new, or different to try to feel not just pleasure, but anything at all.

In the pursuit of pleasure, we pursue more and more things that will at best last only a moment and end up as someone's trash. Chasing these moments is human nature; but it's also the very definition of futility.

To be fair to me, not everything I am collecting and working toward is quite so trite as baseball caps and records. I am also working so that my children and others behind me can live a better life and have access to opportunities to make their lives better. I have worked hard so that my kids could have an education and experiences that will help them in life. I have built a business that I hope will carry on and create great value in the world while providing livelihoods for many people.

Yet, the reality is that I don't know what those people after me will do with all I have tried to create. Will they use the fruits of my labor in ways that are helpful to others? Or will they squander everything I've done and all the opportunities I've tried to create? I have no control over what will happen with what I've worked so hard for.

It can be inspiring to observe some of the great charitable foundations in our country. Men and women who labored and garnered tremendous wealth and then altruistically decided to set aside the incredible sums of money created by their life's work to be used for the betterment of people for generations to come. However, when you look closely at what is happening in many of these philanthropic foundations, you get the feeling that the founder and funder would be disgusted with what's going on. In some cases, future generations with very different values from the older generations are using the funds for things the founder would never have condoned. In many cases, the foundations become simply slush funds to support the lavish lifestyles of the heirs, barely helping the people or causes the funds were originally created to serve.

Regardless of how many lawyers you hire, how specifically you write your will, or how carefully you select who will manage your estate, you cannot control what happens after you die. Everything you worked for will, in the end, be used to satisfy someone else's desires. And you'll never even know what they do because you'll be gone anyway.

But at least you will be remembered for the contribution you made, as you leave a name that will be honored for generations to come. At least people will remember all you did to help others . . .

Uh, no, they won't.

Next time you are driving, look at the names of the streets you pass and notice how many of them are named after people. How many of those people do you know anything about? Have you even heard of them? Did you ever think about the fact that the street was named after a person? To have a street named after you most likely means that you did something important for the community. Not many people get that honor. They must have done something significant that paved the way for the future. And yet here you are, centuries, decades, or maybe only years later, and you know nothing about them.

Yeah, but you are mostly concerned with your family. Strangers may not know you, but your family will know and appreciate what you did for them. Or will they?

Here is a little test. How many of your great-grandparents can you name? You don't have to know full names—first and last will do. In case you need a hint, there are eight of them.

Well, how'd you do?

My guess is that you did very poorly. I like to ask this question of audiences when I speak. It's very unscientific, but I would guess that only about 1 percent of people can name all their great-grandparents. What's worse, many people can't even name one. Think about that—in three generations you will be completely forgotten. After your grandchildren, no one will even remember your name.

Ouch.

No wonder we avoid funerals and thinking about death. The only logical conclusion from thinking about our death is to conclude that everything we work for will be for naught and we will be completely forgotten.

We work and work in an attempt to control the world. Or at least our world. If we can have enough, achieve enough, do enough, then we can prevent things that are painful or harm us. Things that remind us of our mortality.

When tragedy strikes—sickness, accidents, violence—we are reminded that we aren't in control at all. That despite all our efforts, disciplines, diets, exercise routines, precautions, and funds in the bank, the world we live in is chaotic. Order is an illusion. Control is impossible. Times of joy are moments between times of suffering. And there is no avoiding it.

Regardless of your religious background or your view of the afterlife—if there is one and whether your actions in this life impact it—these basic facts about the nature of life and death are inescapable. As the New Testament says, "You are a mist that appears for a little while and then vanishes."[1]

What It Means to Live

What, then, is the point of life? Does it matter what you do if in the end it makes no difference? If we are all going to end up the same way, why make one choice over another? What does it matter how we treat people, how well we do our job, whether we take care of our bodies? Why not, as the old saying goes, just "eat, drink, and be merry for tomorrow we die"?

Coming to the realization that there is ultimately nothing to be gained from life can lead to the conclusion that all the experiences of life are meaningless. However, that realization can also lead to the opposite conclusion. Having a proper perspective of ourselves should give us an immense sense of appreciation for our lives.

How improbable is it that we even exist? How incredible is it that just the right elements came together such that we could inhabit this space and time? How amazing that of all the people everywhere, just the right DNA combined to create you as a person who is totally unique from any other?

Compared to the great expanse of the cosmos, we seem completely insignificant. Relative to the vast scope of time, our life is a blink. And yet right now, in this place and in this moment, we get to experience our life. Regardless of everything else happening in the universe that we will never see or comprehend, we do, in fact, get to experience many wonderful things.

What a gift it is to be able to experience our impact on someone else through a deep relationship. How amazing that we get to see the results of our work, not years after we are gone, but right now in our own lifetime. Despite our inability to know what future generations may do, what a joy it is to see how we can grow and improve ourselves!

Sure, we cannot control what happens after our lives are over. Yet we are given things *during our lives* that are enjoyable. We get to do things that physically feel good—snuggling with our child, finishing a run, or eating ice cream. We get to challenge ourselves and feel the incredible sense of accomplishment of doing something we weren't sure we could do—climbing the mountain, getting the degree, or making the speech. We have the ability to work and achieve and create. We have people in our lives who help us survive, give us comfort, and make us laugh. And we can experience the incredible fulfillment of seeing our efforts truly help someone else.

Despite the fact that it will eventually go away, we get to experience all of those fun, hard, challenging, wonderful things now—today. When viewed through the perspective of our death, our life is something to celebrate. Every moment is worth cherishing. There is meaning even in the seemingly mundane. Irritating situations seem very different when you realize it is a miracle that you are alive to experience irritation (sure the line at the DMV is long, but you are alive and healthy enough to stand in it!). Even tragedy can be appreciated. It's all temporary, which makes savoring it all the sweeter.

Our work, the people we encounter, all the things we see and do—they are all gifts. Not because they help us achieve something, but simply because we have the opportunity to experience them.

To quote minister and author David Gibson:

> When we know that the gift is not meant to be a stepping stone to greater things, when we realize we are not meant to rule the world, or master our destiny, or achieve ultimate gain through our careers, then we discover that enjoyment or joy is itself the reward that we may expect from life and all effort expended in living it . . . There is no surplus to joy beyond joy itself. There is indeed no pathway to joy except by refusing to pursue it and to grasp at it.[2]

As a temporary, soon-to-be-forgotten, yet incredibly unique person, what's the best way to enjoy the gift of your life? Or, said differently, what is your purpose? And how do you live purposely so that you experience that joy?

Living a purposeful life starts with the realization that life is only experienced by the living. You get one shot at it. What you do can never be replicated or relived. It is up to you to choose in each and every moment what that experience will be.

People think about the concept of purpose in many different ways. When I talk about purpose, I simply mean this: how you experience the most joyful version of your life.

To experience a joyful life, you must both understand what personally brings you joy (your purpose) and how to live in a joyful way (doing things on purpose rather than accidentally).

It's kind of a shame that we don't get to experience our own funeral. What we would hear and see could have an impact on how we live in a way perhaps nothing else could. Maybe we should come up with a different ritual that causes us to think about all the questions that our funeral would cause us to ask.

That's kind of what this book is. And the rest of the book is merely an exploration to help you ask, and answer, those questions for yourself.

CHAPTER 2

About Choice

YOU HAVE CHOICES—AN INFINITE number of choices. Too many to comprehend. And you are making choices even when you don't realize it. Here are some statements that frustrate me:

"I don't have time."

As in, "I'd like to read more books, but I just don't have time."

Uh, yeah, you do.

Here's another, much worse one:

"I had no choice."

As in, "I couldn't go to my son's soccer game because I had to work. I had no choice."

Uh, yeah, you did.

When we make statements like these, here is what we are really saying:

"I choose not to spend my time reading books because I would rather be on social media."

And:

"I didn't go to my son's soccer game because I decided to go make money instead."

Of course, when you say it that way, it sounds bad! Worse, it's kind of hurtful! Are you saying I prioritize money over my kids? That I prefer to obsess on the latest conspiracy theory being bounced around social media instead of expanding my horizons through study?

No, I'm not saying that. *You* are. You are saying it through your choices.

No one pried your eyes open with toothpicks and made you look at your phone. Or dragged you away from your child's soccer game at gunpoint and forcefully made you go to work. You chose to use your time that way.

Now, I'm not saying they were bad choices. Maybe you could have watched the soccer game but not had enough money to feed your child when the game was over. Going to work sounds like a good decision. Or maybe you needed some mindless social media distraction to let yourself rest before engaging in something important and taxing. Prioritizing rest for yourself is important. I'm just saying, whatever choices you are making—own them. They aren't dictated by others. They are entirely on you.

Which means you get to control you.

Well, not all of you.

There are many things you have no control over. You can't control where you were born or who your parents are. You can't control your IQ or how athletic you are. You can't control how tall you are or attractive you are (plastic surgery aside). Until we become able to modify our own genetic code, you are stuck with the genes you inherit.

In fact, you can't control most of the things that happen during your life. You can't control the people around you. You can't control their actions or how they feel about you. You can't control the environment you're in, whether there is a rule of law where you live, or if people with power are able to mistreat and abuse others. You can't control nature and its destructive effects—storms, earthquakes, and tornados or bacteria, viruses, and cancers.

But there are other parts of your life, the most important parts, that you control. You decide your actions and your reactions. You choose how and where to put your focus. You decide who you will help or if you will help others at all. You choose how to respond to your emotions. You choose how to spend your energy.

Everyone, regardless of life circumstance, controls these most essential things.

Read that list again and think about that. Regardless of where you live, your physical makeup, how others treat you, what tragedies occur, and even your health, you control how you act and react. Much more on that in the next chapter.

If you are fortunate, you control much, much more. Most likely, you control a whole list of things such as what you eat, where you work, when you work, what you wear, where you live, who you associate with, what you read, what you watch, who you listen to, and who you ignore. The list could go on and on.

Awareness

Think for a moment about how you spend your time. Later in the book, I will suggest an exercise that will force you to really examine this in detail, but for now just think about it at a high level. You do things necessary for survival—sleeping, eating, working. Maybe you do work that you enjoy or maybe not. You almost certainly spend time with other people—your family, your friends. Some of these relationships are enjoyable and some feel more like work. And then you have a little bit of time for yourself—things that you get to do because you enjoy them.

Let's forget for a moment all those "have tos" like sleeping, working, driving our kids to soccer practice, cleaning the house, or cooking dinner. Let's just think about the time we obviously control. Maybe it's after work, on the weekends, after the kids are in bed, or during that brief time in the morning before everyone else is awake. Maybe you choose to be alone or maybe you do something with other people you like. Maybe you do something physical like running or hiking or fishing. Or maybe you chill out and watch the latest streaming series. Maybe you gorge on junk food or go out for drinks with friends.

What is on your activity list? No, really—not the stuff you tell people you do. What do you *actually* do with your time? Have you ever thought about it? Did you purposely decide, "I'm going to choose to lie around watching videos and eating junk food that is going to cause me to get fat"?

The real question is why. Why do you choose to do the things you do? Why do you go to the gym twice a day? Why do you never go to the gym at all? Why do you drink a lot, eat a lot, spend so much time alone, or never spend any time alone? Did you consciously choose those things or did they just kind of happen?

For most of us, most of the time, our choices are unconscious and driven by the most powerful of natural instincts—survival. The survival instinct is arguably the most basic and powerful force on human behavior. For most of human existence, survival was a constant struggle. People had to spend significant portions of their time just trying to provide for their physiological needs—food, water, shelter—and their physical safety—protection from predators.

However, as human societies and technologies have progressed, activities dedicated to providing for our basic physical needs have diminished and left time for other activities. This has left people with more and more time at their disposal to be used in satisfying their other most basic instinct—pleasure.

Pleasure

Interestingly, the pursuit of pleasure is related to our survival instinct. Things that give us pleasure—food, drink, thrills, sex, rest, laughing—do so because they are necessary for our physical or psychological survival. Our bodies reward us with chemicals like dopamine for things we need to do to ensure our species survives. We enjoy these chemicals so much we try to experience them again and again.

Chances are you choose activities that are pleasurable to you. You experience endorphins when you do them or consume them and—whether you're aware of this or not—you continuously chase those endorphin hits.

You don't have to make plans to seek pleasure—it's your natural state because your body rewards it. Here are some things your body might say:

"Hey, I need fuel, so I gotta get this guy to eat. Let's pump him some dopamine when he eats so he'll do it again."

"If this woman doesn't slow down, she's going to wear out. All right, I'll make it feel good to rest so that she'll let me recover."

"Hey, I'm not going to be here forever, and someone's got to take care of me when I'm old. Let's make procreation awesome so this person will want to make others who will help out."

And so on.

However, as we all know, those pleasure chemical hits are intense, but they are also quick. When it's over, what's next? Your body might say:

"Okay, thanks for feeding me. Now back to work."

"Wait, work? Ah, that sounds like too much effort. I want to feel the pleasure thing again. I'll just eat some more."

"You don't need to eat more. I'm full. Wow, you're eating a lot. Well, I guess it's good to have a little stored up for later in case we can't find food for a few days. Okay, here's a little more pleasure chemical."

Due to the incredible abundance in our society, we have choices that were largely unavailable to our ancestors. We have access to seemingly endless supplies of food, drink, and entertainment, and, compared to those ancestors, loads of discretionary time.

As mentioned previously, for most of humanity, days were filled with tasks necessary for survival. Prior to the nineteenth century, 95 percent of humans lived in abject poverty—meaning they hadn't secured the next day's food. Whether they were a farmer who had to continually work to produce food, or a hunter/gatherer who was continually working to find food, everything they did was geared around survival. Overeating wasn't a problem because there wasn't enough food to overeat. And when there was, they had to make it last until they could find their next food source.

In the nineteenth century, the Industrial Revolution took hold, and people started figuring out how to produce things in ways that required much less labor. Suddenly, many people had affordable access to things that used to take them hours of work. By 1900, the number of people in poverty was down to about 80 percent of the population. Cue the twentieth century with its advances in technology and, more importantly, a world full of authoritarian governments with highly structured economies that fell and were replaced with free markets. By the end of the twentieth century, the poverty number was down to 30 percent. In the twenty-first century, the internet and mobile computing arose as more countries joined the wave of capitalism, and now the poverty rate has dropped below 10 percent.[1]

Think about that. For all of human existence—all of those millennia when our bodies were evolving to what we are today—our ancestors lived in a completely different kind of environment. They didn't have a choice as to whether they should spend the day kayaking or lying around watching movies. Their choice was only about what they needed to do that day to ensure survival for them and their family to the next day. We have a strong drive to experience comfort (which is highly pleasurable) because our ancestors developed the instinct to rest whenever they could. They had to spend tremendous effort to survive and had to conserve energy for when food was scarce. Laziness (excessive comfort) isn't an option when the result is starvation.

Have you ever wondered why it's so hard to get up and go to the gym instead of sleeping in? To limit your calorie intake instead of having another piece of pie? It's because your body never developed chemicals to reward the hard stuff. It just assumed you had to do those things.

Delaying Gratification

What, then, would cause people to spend their time doing things that do not provide immediate pleasure or comfort? Philosophers and psychologists have speculated on this for centuries. Aristotle had thoughts (more on that in chapter 4), Freud had his explanation (which certainly involved your mother), and modern psychologists think about it all the time.

There was a now-famous psychological study done in the 1970s that became known as the Stanford Marshmallow Study.[2] The study has been redone in various forms many times over the years, and you may have heard of some version of it. In the original study, preschool-aged children were shown a marshmallow and a pretzel by the experimenter. The children were then told that the experimenter was going to leave the room, and if the child waited for the experimenter to return before eating the marshmallow, the child would get the treat they preferred. If the child didn't want to wait, they could ring a bell and the experimenter would return, but the child would then get the treat that wasn't their favorite.

The results of the original study have been used extensively in developing psychological theories about self-control and delayed gratification. The fun part is reading about the kids' physical manifestations of the excruciatingly difficult waiting (you can watch videos on the internet showing reenactments of the study that are both hilarious and adorable). Hand wringing, singing, pounding the floor, praying. Those poor kids are in agony staring at that delicious-looking marshmallow.

Some researchers followed up years later and observed that the young kids who displayed more self-control in the study ended up outperforming those who showed less self-control in several key metrics such as standardized test scores and social competence. Those who were better able to delay gratification were more likely to demonstrate things like self-confidence and self-reliance.

Later studies have challenged some of the Stanford study's secondary findings. Other researchers have shown that things like standardized test performance and other measures of success are more influenced by other social factors such as the socio-economic status of the child's family and the stability of adult influences. Some posit that those social factors may lead to an increased ability for a child to delay gratification, which is foundational to the child's ability to thrive later.[3]

Whatever your view of the marshmallow study's results, there is one thing that every parent can tell you without the benefit of a double-blind psychological study—delayed gratification is really hard for kids. It is definitely a learned skill and not a natural one. Here's a conversation that's never happened:

Parent to Child: "Would you like a popsicle?"

Child to Parent: "No, I think I should eat my broccoli first."

We have to learn that doing unpleasant, hard, or mundane things now is worth it because it leads to better things later. Sure, broccoli doesn't give a good sugar rush like a popsicle, but it contains the nutrients you need to grow.

In some ways, we are all still the kid who doesn't want to eat our broccoli.

It takes choice and forethought to do the hard things now that will pay off later. Without that forethought, we default to the stuff that gives us the immediate reward. Societies have figured this out and created norms and laws to deter people from actions that will feel good to them in the moment but are harmful to others (and even themselves) in the short or long term.

For instance, many societies have some kind of custom around queuing—determining the order in which people get access to a desired item or activity. It plays out differently in different cultures, but in general there are societally enforced rules that determine who goes next. Exhibit the outrage that occurs when you are waiting to check out at the grocery store, and someone cuts in line. Why are people willing to literally get into a fist fight to enforce a societal norm like a line? We've figured out that the absence of a queuing system creates chaos—when people push and shove to get to the front, inevitably some get hurt and the smaller and weaker ones can't get access. As a society, we have decided that it is good to both avoid fights and protect vulnerable people, so we have created norms for orderly access through queues. This requires that everyone overcome the urge for instant gratification by waiting, instead of shoving aside the old lady who can't find the exact change in her purse.

Surrounded by Choices

I have a friend who spent years studying habits. How are they formed? How long does it really take to make something a habit? I knew that he had planned to write a book to help people understand how to form the good habits that would help them be successful, but the book never came. One day I asked him why he never wrote the book.

"Well," he said. "After all that study, I realized I'm not sure that there is such a thing as a good habit. There are certainly bad habits. But the good things we need to do to be successful? Those never become habitual; they require constant choice."

The good news is that you get to choose what you do. The bad news is that you get to choose what you do. I like this quote from author and journalist Oliver Burkeman:

> We try to avoid the intimidating responsibility of having to decide what to do with our finite time by telling ourselves that we don't get to choose at all—that we must get married, or remain in a soul-destroying job, or anything else, simply because it's the done thing.[4]

This is on you. There is no one else to blame. Whether you read the book or scroll to another post. Whether you sleep in or go to the gym. Whether you stay in the toxic relationship or walk away. Whether your work has meaning or is mere drudgery.

Whether you live a life of purpose or merely a life of pleasure. Whether you live the life you will have wished you had or spend your days feeling regret. You get to choose. Over and over and over again.

Starting right now.

CHAPTER 3

About Creating Your Life

WHEN WAS THE LAST time you stood outside and gazed at the stars and felt in awe? Given the enormity of the universe, you are a speck. A grain of sand in the Sahara.

Forget the universe, how about just our world? I have done a lot of traveling and probably haven't seen a hundredth of a percent of the land on earth (forget the vast oceans). And most places I go, there are so many people.

A few years ago, I drove from downtown Manhattan through Midtown, Harlem, the Bronx, and ultimately out of the city toward Connecticut. The drive took me right through the heart of New York

City. Though I have been to New York many times, it was the first time I had driven that route, and I was struck by the sheer scale. I have lived most of my life in Atlanta, not exactly a small hamlet, and I still couldn't believe we were driving for as long as we were and yet we were still in the city. We weren't in suburbs with single family homes and nice manicured lawns; there was mile after mile after mile of high rises. There are 8.5 million people in New York City. That is roughly the same population as the entire state of Virginia—the twelfth most populous state in the country. And New York packs all of those people into just over three hundred square miles!

Looking at New York from above must be like looking at an anthill after it has been stepped on—there are just people everywhere. Being one out of 8.5 million people who literally eat and sleep on top of each other—how can you help but feel insignificant among that many people?

As I gazed with amazement at this incredible city, it dawned on me—New York isn't even the biggest city in the world. In fact, it isn't even close. It doesn't even make the top twenty-five. Tokyo is the largest at almost five times the size of New York City and is much denser.

Intellectually, I know how many people there are in the world, but seeing such a densely packed city made it real. Compared to the vast number of people in the world, I am incredibly insignificant. Who am I as only one among eight billion people? Why does my life matter at all? How does anyone's life matter?

For centuries, scientists have tried to answer the question as to how life came to be. It is fascinating to see these theories evolve (no pun intended) as we discover new evidence that may imply new conclusions. But while scientists work to answer *how*, they have nothing to say on *why*. *Why* goes into the realm of philosophers. And while you may not be a scientist, you can be a philosopher. At some level, really, you must be.

Creator-Given Purpose

Every choice you make and every action you take has intended consequences. You are doing this to accomplish that. I am eating so that I will be nourished. I am sleeping so that I will be rested. I am calling my mother so that she'll stop nagging me, er, so that I will feel the warmth of a relationship.

Sometimes the actual consequences of our actions don't match the intention. I invested in that stock so that I would earn more money. The stock price went down so that actually I lost money. But the difference in the actual result from the intended one doesn't change the intent.

It is the intention that gives purpose. The purpose of this action is to accomplish that outcome. The same principle holds true for objects. When archaeologists discover things made by ancient civilizations, they ask, "What was its purpose?" The assumption is that if someone expended the time and energy to make something, they must have had a reason to do so. That thing must serve a purpose. Perhaps it was a tool that helped them accomplish a task. Or perhaps it was merely for entertainment.

Biologists view nature through this lens. When discovering a new species of plant or animal, they ask not just how it came to be but why. What role does it play in the ecosystem? As microbiologists learn more about the tiny organisms that form to create human beings, they search to understand the purpose each has in making a human function. We intuitively start with the assumption that each item has a purpose—a result of its being. When one is not obvious, we struggle to explain its existence. We may assume that it evolved to solve a problem that no longer exists. Or we may assume that we simply don't know enough yet to understand its purpose and that eventually after more study we will.

A thing's purpose is given by its creator. That thing could be an object, but it could also be an action—an expense of time and energy. The result desired by the actor or creator gives purpose to the action or item.

The purpose of a drill is to make holes. Centuries ago, someone trying to build with wood figured out that it would be much easier if he had a tool to create holes, so he created a drill. If the carpenter had not needed holes in the wood, then he would not have created the drill. The drill only exists because it had a purpose.

It is this logic—that a thing would not exist or occur if it did not have a purpose—that leads people to believe in a power that created the universe and everything in it. They would argue that the fact that we exist means that something or someone created us, and if something created us then it must have had a purpose in doing so. Therefore, we have a purpose assigned to us by a creator.

Others aren't willing to accept something beyond the physical realm as a possibility, yet still subscribe to this understanding by ascribing nature effectively as the creator. They would argue that natural selection and evolution happen as physical elements strive to survive. And this process causes these elements to change, or to use a different word, create. And each of nature's creations has an intended purpose as it seeks to survive.

If you are to seek purpose in your life, it is vital to understand how purpose works. Things do not come into being unless they serve some purpose. There is a purpose of your being alive. You would not exist otherwise.

You may believe that there is a God who created the universe, had a reason to do so, and therefore has a plan for all of humanity. You may believe God has a specific plan for you personally. Or you may believe that it is an infinite universe trying to expand and survive that created you. Regardless, you were created and therefore you must have a purpose. Your being here is not accidental, incidental, unintended, or inconsequential. If you weren't here, some purpose of God or nature would be left unfulfilled.

Why am I here?

It can be comforting and guiding to understand that there is a higher purpose for being, both for you and all of humanity. Among many other great benefits, looking to the power that created you gives you a perspective and understanding of your own life. Virtually every religion attempts to answer the question "Why are we here?" and scholars spend their entire lives exploring it. I never want to minimize the value of seeking those answers.

However, I would argue that the question "Why are we here?," while helpful, is not a question you actually have to answer. On the other hand, there is a much more important question that everyone *must* answer:

Why am I here?

It is interesting to contemplate the cosmos, but I live here on earth. I'd like to understand why life came into being, but my experience of life is based on how I interact with the people around me. It would be helpful to know why humanity exists, but since I only get to be one person, I am much more interested in what will happen in my life.

Even if you have great clarity and certainty as to the answer to the question "Why are we here?" you are still faced with the problem of how that purpose plays out in your own life. The question "Why am I here?" is something that you have to answer, either consciously or unconsciously. You don't get to choose not to answer that question.

In the last chapter, we explored the things we control and don't control and the choices we get to make about how we spend our time and energy. While there are many things we don't control (where we were born, our physical makeup, the way people around us act, etc.), there are many things we control, and we get to make choices about them. The things we control are much more important than the ones we don't control as they largely determine how we experience our life. Things such as how we respond to our emotions, how we act and react to others, and most importantly, how we spend our time and energy.

In each of these choices, you are the creator of an action. And as creator, you assign purpose to that action.

This is a fine but important understanding, so let's look at it in a slightly different way. The essence of being a living thing is consuming and expending energy. Dead things do neither of these. The fact that you are alive means you are forced to decide what actions you will take as you expend energy. Your life, essentially, is a series of chosen actions.

Every day, you rise and are faced with the question of what you are going to do. What will occupy your time? How will you spend energy? The question you must answer, you have to answer, is what do you want the result of your actions to be? The answer to that question will determine what you choose to do and therefore defines what it means for you to be alive.

Your desired results from your actions—the one thing in your life you control—is your chosen purpose for living.

You have a purpose. The fact that you make any choices at all means that there is a purpose that is causing you to do the things you do. The most important question you can answer is if that subconscious purpose is the one you consciously desire. In other words, when you examine the results of your actions, are they ones that you are glad you will experience? Are they being driven by simple desire for physical pleasure or something else? Are you okay with that?

While you did not cause yourself to become alive, you get to choose what you do during your life. You decide the purpose of those choices, so you are in essence the creator of your life. As the creator of your life, you get to define the purpose of your life.

Before you can begin to think about what actions you should choose to take in your life, you must consider what you want the result of those actions to be. Remember, you don't get to actually control the results—there are too many variables you don't control. But you get to choose the things you do in pursuit of those outcomes.

Repurposing

Earlier, I used the analogy of a drill to illustrate how a creator decides on the purpose of the thing he or she has created. If no one had needed holes, then a drill would have never been created, as a drill's purpose is to make holes.

I have a drill in my workshop. It's a pretty nice drill with a cordless battery and many different bits to attach to it. A few months ago, I decided to build a tree swing for my wife and went out to my workshop to make it. I hadn't been out there for a while (I'm really not that handy), and not far into the project I discovered that the battery for the drill was dead. Not merely without charge, but unable to be charged—dead. Realizing that I was going to have a delay in the project as I went to the hardware store to buy a new drill, I decided to first go through the rest of my tools to see if I needed to get anything else. I soon discovered that my hammer was missing.

"How does a hammer disappear?" I grumbled to myself.

Frustrated, I added "hammer" to my shopping list. As I was preparing to leave, my wife asked me to help her hang a picture.

"I would, but I can't find the hammer."

"How does a hammer disappear?" she asked.

"That's what I said!" I responded. "Wait, I have an idea."

I went back down to the workshop and reappeared with the dead drill.

"What are you going to do with that?"

"Just watch," I said and proceeded to hammer the nail into the drywall using the back of the drill. "Voila." The original purpose of the drill may have been to create holes, but I created a new purpose by using it in a different way. I was the creator of a new use for the drill.

Owning your choices also allows you to recreate them over time. In other words, your purpose—your desired outcome of your choices—can change. When your kids are young, you may choose to prepare meals alone to get some space away from noisy children. When they age, you may ask them to help you cook because meal preparation is a way to spend time together. You can turn a drill into a hammer.

Perhaps the most powerful result of embracing the fact that you choose how you spend your time and energy is that it allows you to own every aspect of your life—even those things that you don't like or were put into your life by someone else.

The story of Joseph from the Bible is one of my favorites. Joseph's brothers couldn't stand him (he was kind of a brat) and so they sold him into slavery (makes how I tortured my siblings seem pretty tame). However, through a string of incredible events, Joseph ends up becoming the number two to Pharoah and rules over Egypt. Later, his brothers come back to him groveling for food and apologizing for what they did. He responds with an incredible phrase:

"What you intended for evil, the Lord intended for good."

Controlling What's Important

Viktor Frankl was born in Austria-Hungary in 1905. He finished medical school in 1930 and immediately began working as a psychiatrist. He opened a private practice in 1937, but, because he was Jewish, had to close it after the Nazis annexed Austria.

In 1942, nine months after getting married, Frankl and his family were sent to a Nazi concentration camp. He spent the next three years in four different concentration camps, including the infamous one at Auschwitz in Poland. During this time, his parents, wife, and brother were all murdered by the Nazis.

After the war, Frankl went on to become a world-renowned psychiatrist, even developing his own concepts that he called logotherapy and existential analysis. His work was foundational in the creation of modern-day positive psychology.

But what Frankl is best known for is a book he wrote in nine days during 1946, not long after being released from the camp. The book was originally titled *A Psychologist Experiences the Concentration Camp* but was later renamed *Man's Search for Meaning*. This seminal work has sold millions of copies and has remained a best seller ever since being published. It certainly had an impact on me.

There are many worthy passages in Frankl's book, but I will quote two of them here:

"Everything can be taken from a man but one thing: the last of the human freedoms—to choose one's attitude in any given set of circumstances, to choose one's own way."[1]

"Man does not simply exist but always decides what his existence will be, what he will become the next moment. By the same token, every human being has the freedom to change at any instant."[2]

No matter what is happening in your life, no matter what has been done around you or to you, you still get to choose how you react, where you put your focus, and how you spend your energy. That cannot be taken from you.

Pause with that for a moment. You control the most important parts of you. No matter what happens to you, you are always in control of what matters. Your actions, reactions, responses, attitude, outlook, focus—those are and will always be in your control. Even things that are evil can be used for good. You can repurpose events in your life. You are the creator of how you experience your life.

The question you must answer is, how do you want to experience life? What are the outcomes you desire from the choices you make?

But let's not try to answer those questions just yet. Before we begin thinking about how we want to experience life, it is important that we pause to make sure we understand some important aspects of our life and, in particular, dispel some misunderstandings that we may have learned.

PART 2:

UNDERSTANDING

"It was her habit to build up laughter
out of inadequate materials."

—John Steinbeck, *The Grapes of Wrath*

CHAPTER 4

About Happiness

IF YOU ASK PEOPLE what they want in life, the answer you most often get is "I just want to be happy."

Thomas Jefferson's well-known words in the Declaration of Independence have become the unofficial purpose statement for Americans: "We hold these truths to be self-evident, that all men are created equal, that they are endowed by their Creator with certain unalienable Rights, that among these are Life, Liberty, and the pursuit of Happiness."

If the pursuit of happiness is at the same level of human rights as my life and freedom, then it must be important. So what makes me happy?

Attempting to answer that question is a lifelong struggle for most people. We don't really understand what happiness is much less how to ensure continual happiness. We have periods where we feel happy and periods where we feel sad, pained, miserable, or just not happy.

We tend to consciously think about our happiness the most when it doesn't feel like things are going well. Every time we are in a struggling relationship, a job we don't like, or practically any unpleasant situation, the question of happiness comes into focus.

Your spouse is being difficult and you're questioning whether you should divorce? I just have to figure out what will make me happy.

Receive some negative feedback from a boss? This job doesn't make me happy anymore.

Get bad service at a restaurant? Inform the manager that I'm not happy.

Though we don't understand happiness, it seems to impact everything from our marriage to our meal to our work. How do we pursue it?

The First Fallacy about Happiness

Ask someone to define happiness and you generally get vague answers. In general, we think of happiness as a feeling or an emotion. We can't explain it, but we think we know it when we experience it.

This isn't a new problem. During the times of the ancient Greeks, Aristotle spent a lot of time trying to understand happiness. He divided happiness into two categories. The first is pleasure—he referred to this type as "hedonic," from *hedonia*, associated with physical pleasures and comfort—food, alcohol, relaxation, entertainment.

When most people describe happiness, they're thinking of only this hedonistic definition. When something feels good, it makes me happy. If it makes me happy, then it must mean I should do it. And since I have an "unalienable right" to happiness, if someone stands in the way of me getting to do something that feels good, then they are violating my rights.

But Aristotle suggested that a sense of happiness comes through a second category as well. He called this second type of happiness "eudemonic," which refers to fulfillment. In contrast to hedonic happiness, eudemonic happiness is associated with the joy felt from the process of fulfilling one's potential and striving for something bigger than one's simple material pleasures.

What was the "something bigger" that Aristotle advocated pursuing? It varied somewhat through his life, but in general, he believed that eudaimonia was experienced in living out one's unique characteristics in accordance with virtue. He mainly advocated for virtues such as reason, wisdom, and understanding, but he allowed for other virtues espoused by philosophers before him like Plato and Socrates—things like temperance, courage, and justice.

In the 1640s, a council of about 150 religious and political leaders from Scotland, England, and Ireland gathered at Westminster. This was during the English Civil War—a tumultuous time in that country's history. Among rather significant topics like who should have the power to rule, the various factions argued about what religion should be allowed in the kingdom and how the government should enforce that religion. The gathered council represented four different views on church government (think denominations), and one of its tasks was to articulate the essential elements of the faith upon which all factions agreed.

In 1647, the Westminster Assembly produced its most famous document. The document consisted of 107 questions and answers, and it was created primarily to be used for instructing children in the Christian faith. Known as the Westminster Shorter Catechism, it was adopted by both the English and Scottish parliaments (maybe the only thing they've ever agreed upon?), though it was later revoked in England when the monarchy was restored following the death of Oliver Cromwell.

The Shorter Catechism is considered by many to be the most accurate and succinct summary of the Christian faith ever written. Though originally intended to be used by children, it has been studied and memorized by scholars over the past centuries. It is most famous for its very first question and answer:

Q. 1. What is the chief end of man?

A. Man's chief end is to glorify God, and to enjoy him forever.[1]

This short statement is packed with theological meaning. Many graduate and doctoral-level divinity students have written extensive studies of its implications. While the theological topics are well worth considering, I think there is a message in this answer instructive to everyone regardless of their faith. At the risk of offending my fellow theologians, please allow me a slightly secularized rephrasing with more modern language:

Question: What is our purpose?

Answer: To pursue something bigger than our self, and subsequently experience great joy in both this life and the one to come.

When it comes to answering the question of what is worth pursuing in life, it is helpful to look at the great philosophers and theologians throughout history. It is no coincidence that so many of them, while living in vastly different eras and coming from very different worldviews, have come to such similar conclusions. Aristotle articulated what people have been discovering for centuries—that pleasure, while wonderful, is both fleeting and depleting. It vanishes quickly and is harder and harder to obtain. However, there are parts of life that bring a sense of happiness that is much more satisfying. Compared to pleasure, these other parts of life lead to effects that are much longer lasting. And unlike merely pleasurable experiences, they are rewarding time and time again.

Unlike pleasure, which is inherently self-focused, all of these more satisfying forms of happiness require focusing on something other than just you.

Let's say that again, differently. If you want to experience the most lasting, satisfying forms of happiness that life has to offer, you must understand the first fallacy about happiness:

It's not about you.

But don't take Aristotle's word for it. Or a bunch of theologians from the Dark Ages. Decide for yourself. Is there a part of you that wants to matter? That longs for proof that your life has meaning? A part that desires some response, some manifestation that gives you certainty that there was an actual result of you having lived?

Do you fear it won't matter that you were here? That you are the tree that fell in the woods that no one heard? That your life isn't just a mist, but a mist that no one else ever knew was there?

Deep in your soul, do you feel like the brief moments of pleasure you experience are becoming more and more hollow? Do you long for something more lasting, more satisfying? Something you don't have to chase again and again, but stays with you?

The only way to satisfy that longing, for your life to matter or to have meaning, to experience happiness that will last beyond a moment, is through your impact on others.

Like a stone dropped into a pond, the ripples that result from you move through other people. The only proof that you exist or ever existed will be based on how you impact others.

Every figure you know from history is only known because of how their actions impacted others. For good or bad, people's actions only take on meaning because they affect others. Think you would have heard of Thomas Jefferson if his words hadn't inspired the founding of a country? Or Hitler if he hadn't murdered millions of people? Or Dr. Martin Luther King Jr. if he hadn't helped so many people gain civil rights? These individuals are only famous because of the impact their actions had on others.

And you are no different. If you are interested in a life that matters, you must decide how you want to impact others.

Pause on that thought.

A life that matters, the meaning of your life, the proof that you were here, your impact on the world, your imprint, how you know you are alive—choose whichever phrase resonates with you. The reality is that the results of your life can only be measured, observed, or proven by the fact that your existence altered the course of the people you encountered. Sure, you have some purely personal experiences (and they are often worth cherishing), but there will be no evidence of those. If you want proof that your life meant something, you can only look at what you are doing to or for other people.

All of us have some inherent longing to matter. Only some of us learn that the only way to fulfill that desire is by doing things that impact others.

Hedonia, or the pursuit of pleasure, is an incomplete fulfillment of happiness. If only subconsciously, we all understand our temporal boundaries. We know we will only occupy a limited space and time, yet we desire to expand that by being a part of something bigger. Left solely on our own, pleasure quickly fades, and we feel incomplete. But by being in relationships and doing things that impact others, we can expand beyond our physical boundaries and become something more.

Doing things that impact others provides a more lasting sense of happiness because it solves a psychological need that isn't dependent on quickly dissolving hormones in our brain. It satisfies more deeply seeded desires that create satisfaction, which lasts much longer than any endorphin hit ever could.

While happiness is a vague state of mind that is difficult for us to explain, predict, or define, to understand it *we must start by rejecting the first fallacy about happiness—that happiness is about us*. Happiness is completely about others. Not what others do to or for us, but what we do to or for them.

Paradoxically, the more focused you are on yourself, the less happy you will be.

It is one of life's great ironies that the way to experience happiness is to focus not solely on yourself, but on what you can do for others.

The Second Fallacy about Happiness

Since our founding, Americans have taken pride in our work ethic and ingenuity. We aren't just pursuing happiness, but the "American Dream." And that dream consists of not just great material wealth, but the security that comes with it.

The United States still provides a unique culture and environment for people to climb the socio-economic ladder. We live in a place where an individual who is willing to work hard and take risks can achieve great accomplishments and earn wealth well beyond his or her predecessors. Where, at least compared to many societies, one's limits for achievement are much more to do with one's personal choices than the station in life they inherited.

There is one thing that nearly every wealthy, accomplished person will tell you—that when they fulfilled the dream and got to the top of the ladder, they . . . wait. No, that never happens. There is no top of the ladder. What people who have earned a lot of wealth will tell you is that as they climbed the ladder what they found was more rungs. There is no end to what you can achieve or earn. There is never "enough." There is no destination.

All of us have felt the high of achievement. Maybe it was after a graduation, a promotion, or a purchase. You worked so hard to reach a goal and then when the emotions wore off, you felt empty. You realized that all your time and energy spent toward that single goal yielded a moment of exhilaration and then . . . nothing. You felt the same. Or maybe, realizing that the object of your focus was over, you felt lost.

Pleasure is fleeting, but so is everything else. Anything we achieve, earn, or experience in this life is momentary. Even great acts of service we do for others won't be remembered. The feeling we get from achieving the thing will only last a moment and then we will be left asking, "Now what?"

Regardless of where you are on life's ladder—you will never reach a point where you are done. Where all your desires have been met. Where you want for nothing. The pain, insecurity, or frustration you feel won't disappear through an achievement. Whatever climbing the next rung means to you—more financial security, more independence, or more recognition—may be absolutely worthy of pursuit as you attempt to improve the circumstances of your life. However, you must realize that, even if you realize them, those circumstances you are pursuing will be temporary. If your happiness is contingent on a certain set of circumstances—financial, relational, or physical—then that happiness will go away as soon as those circumstances change. And that change is inevitable.

To understand happiness, we must understand and *reject the second fallacy—that happiness is dependent on external circumstances.*

Our struggle with the fallacy of the conditionality of happiness warps our view of our present and our future. If my happiness is conditioned on my circumstances, then how can I be happy if I am poor? How can I be happy when I hate my job? How can I be happy if I'm in an unhealthy relationship?

Assuming that those circumstances are responsible for us being unhappy, we set ourselves up for the disappointment of still not being happy when our circumstances change. We work and work to change our conditions, only to be bewildered once our conditions change and our happiness hasn't.

"I thought that if I got this job, I would be happy."

"I thought that if I ended that relationship, then I would be happy."

"I thought that if I just moved, then I would be happy."

Yet once we have the next job, or change our relationship status or where we live, the dust settles and we feel the same.

The only way of experiencing happiness is to choose it in each and every moment, regardless of what is happening in our life.

Wait, stop. That last sentence sounds an awful lot like a meme or some cheesy motivational speaker's advice. Before we roll our eyes and move on, let's pause and actually think about that statement: The only way of experiencing happiness is to choose it in each and every moment, regardless of what is happening in our life.

As Viktor Frankl taught us, even in life's worst circumstances, we are still in control of the most important parts of ourselves; we can control our thoughts and attitude. Despite our circumstances or what others may or may not have done to or for us, we get to choose the mindset we will have regarding that situation.

But if you are like me, it may still feel tough to make this practical and not just motivational-poster gobbledygook. If happiness isn't something I achieve, but rather something I must choose every day, how do I actually do that?

Let's set aside the idea of happiness for a moment and look at this differently. What choices can we actually make in each circumstance? Let's consider some other concepts.

Contentment, Gratitude, Joy

While I may not be exactly sure what it is to be happy, I can understand what it means to be content. Contentment is when I have decided that what I have is sufficient. Contentment releases me from the illusion that further accumulation is needed to make me whole. That there is something else out there that isn't fleeting. I may not know how to choose to be happy, but I can choose to be content.

How about satisfaction? Satisfaction is when I decide not to pursue more. It means I have chosen the end of the journey. I have consciously chosen to free myself from a treadmill of effort that takes me nowhere. I'm not quite sure how to choose happiness, but I can choose to be satisfied.

Contentment and satisfaction are related but different. If I am at a meal, contentment means that I decide that the amount of food I have is enough for what I need. Satisfaction is deciding not to try to get more food.

Perhaps most importantly, consider gratitude. Gratitude is more than being thankful—it is the value of choosing to look for things to be thankful for. It is the discipline to find the gift in every circumstance.

As I was sorting through how to write this chapter, I had a conversation with a friend whom I consider to be wonderfully wise on this topic. Ironically, I was late to the meeting with her because I had to first take my son to soccer practice but was delayed on the way to the field as the highway was shut down by a wreck. So he was late to practice and I was late to our meeting.

Starting the conversation, I (sort of) joked about how challenging it is to choose to be happy while you are sitting on a highway unable to move and knowing that your tardiness will cause problems for others.

She replied, "Oh, that would be easy."

"What do you mean?" I replied.

"That would be an easy moment as there are so many things to be grateful for. First, I would be so grateful that it wasn't me or someone I love in that wreck. Second, I would be grateful that I was in a warm car with enough gasoline in the tank. Third, I would be grateful for the extra time with one of my children. That's such a gift. I could name several more. You just have to look at the gifts in the situation."

Gratitude isn't merely looking for the silver lining. It's understanding that every experience in life is a gift—meaning it was something given to you by someone else. Gratitude forces us to look for the factors in our circumstances that we did not earn or create and so admit to ourselves our inadequacy and fallibility. Gratitude allows us to recognize gifts and therefore enjoy them. We aren't promised another day or even another breath. The fact that we get to be in this time and space with these people is a miracle.

Contentment, satisfaction, gratitude. These are tangible—I understand what they mean. I can develop the discipline to contemplate them in any situation. But isn't there still some element of emotion in happiness? Some feeling that is associated with it?

Psychologists would call that feeling joy.

When we say we want to "feel happy," joy is the emotion we are describing. Joy is a feeling of great pleasure. We think of joy as delight or elation. Joy is an emotional expression that is a reaction to success in obtaining something you desire. We don't use the term "joy" very often in our society, but when we do it is often in a phrase such as "he had a look of pure joy on his face." We associate joy with children seeing what Santa left under the tree or getting to meet Mickey Mouse for the first time.

Joy is a feeling that some of us have forgotten. As adults, we have been too exposed to the realities of a harsh world. Gone are the joyful innocent novelties of childhood—our days are filled with the drudgery of survival. Perhaps that is why we are so intent on the pursuit of objects, achievements, and anything new—we are seeking even a moment with the feelings of joy we experienced when we were younger. No wonder we despair when those wonderful feelings slip from us so quickly.

If joy is the emotional reaction to obtaining something you desire, the way to feel joy is to either obtain more or desire less.

A magical thing happens when we choose contentment, satisfaction, and gratitude. Suddenly the circumstance you are in is all you want. You have no desire to chase more. You are so grateful to have been given so much. You realize that your circumstances are in fact so desirable that you feel . . . joy.

This brings us back to talking about choices. I can choose to be content and decide that what I have is enough. I can choose to be satisfied and not pursue more that will inevitably leave me empty. I can exercise the discipline to find the gifts in a situation. And by choosing to do these things, I can choose to be joyful.

When feeling joy is based on my choice, then I get to experience it again and again. Once I am released from the fallacy that joy, the feeling of happiness, is based on something or someone else, then I am in complete control of when I feel joy.

Putting It Together

These two fallacies may seem somewhat contradictory—happiness isn't about us, yet it isn't caused by our circumstances. Said affirmatively, happiness is found in what we do for others and choosing it regardless of circumstances.

The lessons are simply this: The most satisfying things in life— the things that last beyond a moment—are found in serving others. Everything else is fleeting and ultimately unsatisfying and so therefore unable to make us happy. Knowing this, we can choose to be joyful in every circumstance.

It is because I control my joy that I define purpose as how I experience the most joyful version of my life and not the happiest version. I can understand what it means to be joyful, which means that in a given moment, it is easier for me to choose to be joyful than it is for me to choose to be happy.

I have found that many people have the same challenges with the ideas of happiness that I do. These truths about happiness run counter to most everything we are told by our society. We have so much baggage from years of misinformation on the subject. Countless advice from friends, family, and marketing people telling us that if we only had this or got rid of that we would be happy has scarred us. It is for this reason also that I have begun to talk about a purposeful life as a joy-filled life instead of a happy one.

There is only a small distinction, but sometimes simply using new language can be helpful.

You may be comfortable focusing on your happiness instead of joy. This is about you not me, so do whatever works for you. The important thing is that your quest to be happy or to experience joy is caused by applying these disciplines to your life—serve others and be grateful. Those are the keys.

CHAPTER 5

About the Journey

FOR TEN YEARS, I was active in triathlon—races that include swimming, biking, and running. I spent a considerable amount of time training, with months spent building up to big races. There is nothing like the feeling of elation experienced just after crossing the finish line in a race you have spent hundreds of hours training for. The psychological feeling of accomplishment combined with the physical endorphins is absolutely exhilarating.

For a few hours.

And then you hit the point later that day (or if you are lucky the next day), when the emotions and hormones fade, and you realize that the major focus of your life for months or even years is over.

And all you are left with is wondering if it was worth it—and then trying to figure out what happens next.

One year toward the end of my triathlon "career," I was training for a big race. It was by far the most dedicated I had ever been, and I was absolutely in the best shape of my life. Two weeks before the race, I did a long training session where I absolutely smoked my pace goals for the race. I was incredibly confident and excited about a potential finish well above what I had ever achieved before.

Then, three days later, about ten days before the race, I was on an easy training ride with friends and got into a bad accident. My collarbone was shattered, and I had displaced ribs and horrible road rash.

As the reality of the situation hit me, I got really down emotionally. No race. I would never get to show my friends and family what I could do. Worse, I realized that even when I recovered, I didn't think I could go through the level of training I had endured that year again. It was not only taxing on me but also on everyone around me. I had an important job and a family with young kids. To do that kind of training required sacrifices from both my colleagues and my family. I just didn't think I could ask them to go through it again.

Lying on the recliner that served as my bed for the next several weeks, I began to recognize that the races weren't actually the goal of my involvement in triathlon. Nothing magical happened on race day. All of the things that I desired from triathlon—the results I wanted to experience in my life—almost all of those were a result of the training. It was the training that shaped my body, made me feel energetic, helped me develop discipline, and put me in a situation to be competitive. The training was where the magic happened—the race was merely a celebration to demonstrate what the training had done.

As I lay there in pain, I realized that I was still in the best shape of my life (shattered clavicle aside). I had proven to myself that I could sustain the discipline of high-level training. And even though

I wasn't able to prove it to anyone else, I knew what I was capable of doing. And unlike post-race endorphins, those things weren't going away anytime soon. For the rest of my life, I would enjoy the confidence the training created. Despite the pain, I felt incredible.

The accomplishment isn't in the moment of finishing a race—of cashing the check, buying the car, or marrying the girl. Those things are merely milestones that signify where all the real reward comes from. The long string of hard, tiring, frustrating, painful efforts is what creates the desired state. And understanding that reveals the joy of the journey.

It's been several years since I raced in a triathlon. There may be a time when I do it again, but my current season of life has me choosing other activities instead of going on three-hour bike rides. I still train—though not like I used to; but my understanding of what training does for me has created a love of the discipline and effort required to exert myself in daily exercise. Every time I am out of breath during a run or straining to do another pushup, I am grateful for the struggle.

Joy in the Journey

Choosing to be content (what I have is enough) and to be satisfied (I am not pursuing more) could imply that we stop working. After all, if I am content with what I have, then what is the point of trying to get more? Doesn't being content mean that you stop trying? If I am content with my job, shouldn't I stop doing the hard work required to get another job? If I am content with my relationships, doesn't that mean there is no need to expend the effort of investing in them further? If I am content with who I am as a person, doesn't that mean I no longer need to expend the energy required to improve myself?

If I am choosing to be satisfied with what I have and not pursuing more, that means I get to relax, right?

In fact, it's just the opposite.

Every year, my daughter and I assemble a puzzle together over the Christmas holidays. We sit for hours, working and singing along to cheesy music. In the end, we have this work of art displayed on the table for the rest of the family to admire.

But only for a few days. Then it's time to put up the Christmas decorations, at which point the puzzle is unceremoniously torn apart and put into a box in a closet never to see the light of day again. The result of our hours and hours of labor is destroyed mere days after its completion. We have an unspoken agreement that my wife will destroy the puzzle when my daughter and I aren't around. It's too painful to watch.

So why do we continue these futile labors year after year, knowing that each time our end product will so quickly be discarded? Because the point is in the work, not the results. It's the time working together that is special, not a picture distorted by a thousand curved lines.

When you are no longer consumed by futile efforts aimed at chasing nonexistent rewards, you are left with a tremendous amount of time and energy at your complete disposal. You are presented with an endless number of choices as to how to best experience the most lasting, most rewarding things that life has to offer. You get an opportunity to utilize your unique design and desires in a way that generates substantial value as demonstrated in your experiences and in the lives of others. You are granted an awareness that every moment and every effort is to be appreciated as a part of that journey.

You may work harder than you've ever done. You may invest more time in relationships, even difficult ones. You may devote even more energy into personal passions that help you grow. But instead of doing all of these things in a vain pursuit of nonexistent rewards, you will do so with the understanding that all of that work is itself rewarding. That every action is both a means and an end—your activities may lead to potential rewards, but mostly, like building a puzzle, they are simply to be cherished themselves.

When you are choosing to live the most joyful version of your life, it opens your eyes to the many things that can be joyful. Being consciously aware of your choices allows you to choose the things that are most meaningful to you. But it also helps you see the meaning in activities that you've never seen before.

Seeking to live joyfully leads to deep fulfillment—both because one is doing fulfilling things and because they see the meaning in the things they do. An attitude of joy may or may not change the things we choose to do, but it will certainly change how we perceive the things we are doing.

Recently, I was cleaning up the kitchen after a meal with my family. Cleaning the kitchen is not on my list of deeply meaningful activities. I'm not passionate about it, nor am I particularly good at it, and it's not going to deeply impact anyone's life. I don't remember anyone's eulogy including wording about how good they were at washing dishes.

As I stood there silently fuming about doing a chore that felt like such a waste of time, I looked up and saw my teenage kids, who were still in the kitchen talking after dinner. My first thought was, "Why don't I get the kids to do this instead of me? I mean, I'm in charge here and I can still order my kids around." (Well, I'd like to think that anyway.)

Then I thought about the importance of my relationship with my kids and the things I want to teach them that will make them healthy adults who are able to have great relationships with others. Things like humility, sacrifice, service, discipline, and caring. It dawned on me that the best way for me to teach them humility wasn't to tell them about it but to demonstrate it. If even Dad does the dishes, then that must mean that no job is beneath any of us.

My whole attitude changed in that moment. I immediately went from frustration to, well, joy. Not because I suddenly started enjoying dish washing, but because I saw the purpose of it. That act of service was a part of helping me accomplish my life purpose as expressed through my relationship with my kids.

This is a small and rather insignificant example, but I have found that the philosophy holds, even for bigger and harder things in life.

Releasing yourself from the lie that happiness resides at a destination allows you to experience the joy that is possible during the journey. The things that alter your life, that make you who you are, are the result of the millions of steps along that journey. Awareness of that allows you to choose joy in every moment and circumstance.

You may be thinking that it is easy for someone like me to say things like this because I don't know the extent of your struggle. You may not be trying to get to the next rung on the ladder but merely the first rung. Your pain may not be from trying to achieve something great but merely trying to survive. Maybe it's not just life in general that has hurt you, but specific people. Perhaps people you should have been able to trust have abused you, and you think I couldn't possibly understand.

Certainly, we must reach a place where our most basic physical and psychological needs are being met before we can even think about more lofty things. It is not only worthwhile but also necessary and moral to work to escape dangerous or abusive situations and put ourselves in a place where we can not only survive but thrive. To tolerate unhealthy situations betrays the very value of our life. The fact that we can choose joy in suffering is by no means a reason to tolerate the causes of suffering.

As we seek to live a life of purpose—experiencing our most joy-filled life—we will inevitably identify circumstances we need to change and people we need to escape. Yes, we can choose joy in the worst circumstances. No, we cannot use even the most toxic relationships as an excuse to not find joy in life, but life is hard and there are plenty of difficult things and people that we must endure. There is nothing ignoble about avoiding the ones that we can.

On the contrary, the more our understanding of what is worthwhile in life grows, the more benefit there is to us and others to seek it. When we know the things that are truly rewarding involve using our time, talent, and treasure in a way that serves others and our future self, seeking those activities is a moral response. When we enjoy things that benefit others and ourselves, we should try as often as possible to do things we enjoy!

While there are plenty of us who are in unhealthy circumstances or relationships that are difficult to escape, what I often see are people who are in unhealthy circumstances or relationships who don't realize it or who have given up on trying to change them.

Becoming conscious about our purpose opens our eyes to the choices we are making today and forces us to reevaluate them. That evaluation almost always results in some kind of change—sometimes a change in the way we see what we are choosing to do and sometimes changing what we do.

We are all wired differently. The things I enjoy, desire, and am good at are different from what you enjoy, desire, and are good at. The values and principles that I want to apply in my life are not the same as yours. The way I prefer to spend my time, the way I desire to approach relationships, what I hope for my kids all of these things are unique to me. To apply them in my life, to choose what I want to do and not to do, I need to understand what all those unique attributes and beliefs are. I need to understand what I really enjoy. If I want to ensure I make joyful choices and not just leave my life to chance, I need to make conscious choices. Which means I need to spend time understanding me.

CHAPTER 6

About Your Formula

MY WIFE IS AN amazing person; she's my soul mate and my best friend. She is creative and an amazing designer. She can walk into a room and see what the space could become and the emotions it can evoke.

She is also really weird.

Several years ago, we were out together and walked into a store we had never seen before. As we entered, her face lit up and she gasped. Inside this small store were tables covered with bin after bin filled with antique doorknobs and hinges. Thousands and thousands of them. They were in no discernable order. It was just wall-to-wall random assortments of old door hardware.

I knew that I had lost her for the next couple of hours as she dove in elbow-deep at the first table. She was in heaven.

I was in hell.

I cannot fathom how picking through boxes full of old junk can possibly be enjoyable. I really don't ever want to buy a doorknob, but if I did, I would go to the local hardware store where they are sorted so that one can easily find the size they need. Just looking around that place made my shoulders and neck tense up. I had to leave.

"Call me when you're done. I'll be . . . somewhere else."

"Uh-huh," was her barely discernable response. I no longer existed.

When we did reconnect, she was ebullient. "The artistry of those hinges is amazing. Each of them had such personality. Entering a room and feeling a doorknob like that in your hand would totally prepare you for a different experience."

I didn't dare ask her to elaborate on the personality of a hinge.

Her weirdness doesn't stop there. One of my favorite things to do when we travel is to go for an early morning run so I can see the area where we are staying. You really get a unique perspective when you are on foot compared to being in a car. And starting my day with the endorphins of a run feels amazing.

"I don't understand why you like to run. It's so hard and boring."

"What do you mean? It's not boring! I get space to think, and the endorphins make me feel great all day!"

How am I married to this person?

The joy I get from running and the joy she gets from, er, doorknobs, come from the same place—an awareness of our unique makeup and the deliberate choices we make to put ourselves in positions to do things that feed us. We share a desire to live a joy-filled life, but the way we live that out isn't the same.

All of us have a purpose, but our individual purposes aren't the same. Each of us has a unique makeup that was created in a unique context. It's an amazing experience of life that we get to discover and decide our individual purpose. The more we know about ourselves, the more we are able to make choices that will give us joy.

One could argue that we all do this intuitively anyway. I don't have to do a lot of self-discovery to understand that I like ice cream. When I get access to ice cream, I eat it because I enjoy it. I don't need times of deep thinking to figure out that I love spending time with my kids. They are awesome and I just like doing fun things with them.

But most choices in life aren't as straightforward as knowing you like dessert or spending time with your kids. Choices always involve tradeoffs—that's what makes it a choice. I can do this or that. I can go this direction or that direction. If I am saying yes to this, it means I am saying no to that. The older you get and the more responsibility you have, the harder these tradeoffs get. There are fewer and fewer clear-cut issues. Few things are black and white, and many more of them are gray. Rarely are choices matters of good and bad, but normally between bad and worse or (hopefully) good or better.

Here are some examples:

- My boss is offering me an opportunity to work on a new project. It could lead to advancement down the road, but it will be a lot of work to get up to speed as I learn new skills and will mean less time at home. Do I accept it?

- I have job offers from two different companies—one is a startup, and one is a more established business. Which do I take?

- I have two children who both have extracurricular events at the same time in different places. Which one do I attend?

- I have a rare free afternoon alone when no one needs me. How I spend it is completely at my own discretion. What should I do?

- I have a friend who is exhibiting behaviors that are hurting her relationships. If I say something to her, it will almost certainly offend her and endanger our friendship. Should I talk to her?

I could come up with an endless number of examples—and so could you. In fact, I would bet you have something that is coming to mind right now. We are constantly faced with choices that involve tradeoffs. Yes, I like ice cream, but I also like being able to fit into my pants!

It depends . . .

Imagine for a moment that it isn't you facing these decisions, but a friend who comes to you for advice. It's probably not very hard for you to imagine this, because it has most likely happened—if not about one of these exact scenarios, then about something very similar. My guess is that more than likely, your answer to your friend is the same answer I give to others who ask me for advice.

"It depends."

When someone asks me for advice on what they should do, I usually preface those two words with, "Well, you're not going to like my response, but *it depends*."

Recently I had a conversation with a lady who started her own business a few years ago. She has put in a lot of hard work and over the past two years the business has really started to grow. Not surprisingly, she has started getting calls from investment bankers telling her she could sell her business. She hired one and they quickly had a few companies who were interested.

She called and told me about the situation and asked, "Do you think I should sell?" And guess what I said . . .

"Well, it depends."

It depends on how you want to spend your time. Do you enjoy

doing what you do, or are you tired of it and want to try something else? Are you satisfied with what you've achieved, or do you feel like you still have things you want to do? Do you feel like you are capable of leading the business through the next phase, or do you think someone else is better suited to that? Do you want to have someone else as a boss who can support you, or do you want to keep calling the shots?

She was in a tremendous position with no bad choice. Selling her company meant taking a significant payout that she could spend and invest in other places. Keeping it meant she would have a long-term income stream. The decision really came down to how she wanted to live her life and spend her time. And that question takes a lot of self-reflection.

One of my favorite movie scenes is from the Disney animated classic *Alice in Wonderland*. In the scene, Alice is lost as she walks through the woods when she comes upon an area with signs pointing in various directions with labels like, "Up, Back, This Way, Yonder."

"Now, let's see. Where was I?" Alice says. "I wonder which way I ought to go."

It is then that the Cheshire Cat appears. The cat is a frustratingly strange creature, able to disappear and reappear, remove his ears like he is tipping a cap, and continually sings a strange tune. He starts to leave almost as quickly as he has appeared, but Alice stops him.

"Oh wait! Don't go, please!" Alice protests. "I just wanted to ask you which way I ought to go."

The cat responds, "Well, that depends on where you want to get to."

"Oh, it really doesn't matter . . . ," Alice replies.

To which the cat points out, "Then it really doesn't matter which way you go!"

Most of us aren't faced with the question of whether we should sell our business for millions of dollars, but all of us are forced daily to make decisions that will impact us today and in the future.

Making those decisions requires us to know where we want to get to. Recognizing that there is no ultimate destination, it really means we need to know how and where we want to be.

What is my desire for how I spend my time? How I make a living? How I interact with others? How would I describe the relationship I desire with my family and friends? How do I hope to feel physically? How do I want others to think of me? How do I want to respond to crises or tragedies?

The answer to these questions and the millions of others we face are unique to each of us. Our desire for the outcome of each choice—what we want the experience of our life to be—is a result of all the things that make us uniquely us.

In this section, we have explored fallacies about happiness and concluded that rather than subjecting us to the conditional notions of happiness, the better path is to choose things like contentment, gratitude, and joy. We have also begun to understand that rewards in life come not from a destination or achievement, but in choosing joy during every step of life's journey. The individual choices we make along that journey are a reflection of what makes us uniquely us.

How do we gain a good enough understanding of ourselves to confidently choose what we want the experience of our life to be? There are many things that go into forming our individual set of desires for how we live life. In general, the lens through which we see decisions—and the outcomes we hope for—comes from what I call our unique formula. The ingredients of this formula blend from three general areas. It is a mix of our passions (the things that stir us), our strengths (our mix of talents and capabilities), and our legacy (the impact we desire to have on our future self and others).

In the next section, we will spend time reflecting on each of these in depth.

PART 3:

REFLECTION

"I may not be as strong as I think, but I know
many tricks and I have resolution."

—Ernest Hemingway, *The Old Man and the Sea*

CHAPTER 7

About Passion

I HAVE ALWAYS LOVED music but didn't start learning to play an instrument until I was an adult. I was able to become a passable guitar player, but never became as good as I would have had I started playing before I took on adult responsibilities. Similarly, my wife, who is also a talented vocalist, began learning the piano as an adult. Both of us wished that we had started playing earlier, but neither of our parents had a strong passion for music and it was never really offered to us. Still, despite our mediocre skills as instrumentalists, we have a great love for music and believe it has many benefits. It is a wonderful creative outlet, something that can be done both alone and with others, and, unlike many other activities, can be enjoyed throughout life.

Because of this, we decided when our kids were young that each of them would learn to play the piano. Not only is piano a wonderful instrument for enjoying and writing music, but it is also a fantastic way to learn music theory that can be applied to any other instrument.

So yes, we were the parents that forced their kids to take piano lessons. Spare me your judgment.

As you can imagine, our three very different children reacted to the piano very differently. They went through various phases of embracing, tolerating, and totally rejecting their lessons. Sometimes they moved back and forth between these within a month.

If you are a parent, you have had to deal with the consequences of the ultimatums you set for your kids. They'd better be important, because often the consequences are worse on you than the child:

You say: "You are not getting out of that chair until you eat your vegetables."

Two hours later you can't go to bed because you are in a staring contest with an amazingly stubborn three-year-old.

You say: "If you miss another homework assignment, you are losing your driving privileges."

The next week you are late to work because you have to drive your seventeen-year-old to school.

There were many times where my wife and I regretted making piano a requirement in our house, because it meant we had to deal with forcing our kids to practice. We set timers, gave constant reminders, and doled out an occasional punishment when lessons were missed. Time and again we questioned whether all the struggle was worth it, but since we had created the rule, we had to see it through.

It was funny though, because we never had to set alarms for softball practices or soccer games.

When you are passionate about something, you don't need an external source to motivate you to do it. Passion provides a seemingly endless source of energy. Passionate runners will look for any opportunity to go for a run. Someone who is only running because their doctor told them they need to lose weight is going to require a lot of extra motivation and self-discipline.

Our passions germinate from different places and change over time. Some passions are the result of things that happen to us early in life. Some derive from ideas we deeply believe in. Most often passions develop out of significant life experiences, sometimes positive but many times tragic.

Childhood

One of the things that good pre-marital counselors do is to help each partner understand the expectations they have of how a marriage should work. For better or worse, these are generally shaped by the way we saw our parents behave.

We have some good friends who talk about how this played out in their marriage. One of them came from a very traditional home where the mother kept the house and managed the kids, and the father would come home from work every day so the whole family could sit down together for dinner. The other partner came from parents who divorced right after having kids. The parents lived far from each other, worked, and were in and out of many relationships. There was not only no such thing as family dinner, but it was up to each person to figure out what they were going to eat.

This led to some humorous (in hindsight) situations early in their marriage as one person waited at home with a rapidly cooling, home-cooked meal while the other one obliviously worked late. It also led to some not-so-humorous arguments about respect and communication.

Each of us has closely held values that are generally shaped at a very early age. Values are those principles that hold great worth to us. They are so important that when we act in accordance with them, we feel whole and at peace, but when we act against them, we feel discord and even guilt.

We also have beliefs that shape our behavior. Beliefs are the ideas that we hold to be true or that we think work to get the outcomes we desire. Some of our beliefs are more like preferences—we think they are true, but we are okay with deviating. I believe that mint chocolate chip ice cream is the best, but I'm okay if you get me strawberry instead. But some beliefs we hold so closely that they shape our behavior almost as much as values—it would take a lot to convince us they aren't true. Some of our beliefs are formed as we see things happen around us—watching the results that actions or situations have on others. Generally, our most closely held beliefs, those we are really passionate about, come from things that happen to us.

My grandparents were some of the kindest, most generous people I have ever known. They were also some of the thriftiest. Instead of buying Ziploc bags, my grandmother would store food in reused bread bags closed with the also reused wire. Their incredibly overstuffed storage closet/pantry/laundry room was like a museum of old consumer items stored in antique cracker cans and cigar boxes. Don't even mention the attic.

These wonderful people grew up in rural Alabama and Tennessee during the Great Depression. One time when I was a teenager, I visited the farm that my grandfather grew up on. The farm was owned by one of his siblings who had built a home on the front part of the property. During the visit, my grandfather took me on a walk to the back part of the farm to see the old, abandoned shotgun house that was his childhood home. He talked about how hard farming was, how often they missed or barely ate meals, and how many of his family members couldn't find work.

Missing meals as a child is an experience that leaves an impression. So is seeing how the adults in your life work to make sure you don't miss more of them. The experiences of their childhood gave my grandparents a strong value of hard work. It also gave them the belief that you should save everything you can because you don't know when you are going to need it.

It is hard to underestimate the impact that our childhood has on the values and beliefs that drive us. For some, our core values come from loving parents who imparted them to us through years of caring and guidance. We have such a strong connection with the security and comfort of those relationships that the fundamental ideas they gave us at an early age become the bedrocks of our belief system.

For others, values were instilled by parents who, though perhaps well meaning, exhibited self-destructive behaviors that we learned. Having adapted to the environment of our childhood, we now exhibit those same behaviors because we are tragically comfortable in the chaotic environment they create. When challenged about actions we take that hurt ourselves and others, we angrily defend them.

For still others, we react to childhood trauma by rejecting the beliefs and behaviors that created it and passionately pursue the opposite.

My father grew up in the poorest areas of Atlanta. He never knew his father, and his mother was an alcoholic who worked as a waitress when she was sober. They were constantly moving from place to place, mostly moving in with whatever man she was seeing at that time. When he was twelve years old, his mother showed back up to their public housing unit after having disappeared for three days on a bender. His uncle (who had been paralyzed after being stabbed in a bar fight) cashed his disability check to pay for my father's taxi ride to the Department of Child Services. He spent the next few years in orphanages and foster care, ultimately living with a loving family who completely changed his life.

He often tells the story of the first time he was in his foster family's home, and they sat down to dinner together. They all sat at the table patiently and waited for their mother to sit, the father prayed, and then they talked and laughed as they ate. He had never experienced or seen anything like it. He just knew he loved it.

As an adult, he sought to live a life that was the total opposite of what he saw in his childhood. He got married and had kids very young, because he wanted a family to create dinner table experiences of his own. He worked hard so that there would always be plenty of food and a place to live. And he never touched alcohol.

Childhood experiences don't have to define us, but they certainly influence us. Understanding how can be powerful.

Influences

I have had a lot of teachers. Going through elementary, middle and high school, then college and graduate school, I estimate that I had at least 120 different teachers. This doesn't include various coaches, instructors, pastors, and music or theater directors.

I so appreciate anyone who chooses education as a career. It is a selfless decision and a high calling—to spend your life serving others through teaching them. And I am incredibly grateful for all the teachers I had through the years. They were a part of making me who I am today.

Now, having said that, I will say something that will offend many of my former teachers: I don't remember many of them.

Ouch. I know. Terrible. I mean, if someone showed me a picture, I'm sure I would have some recollection—that memory has to be in my brain somewhere. But before you get too offended, be honest with yourself: Do you remember all the teachers you ever had?

See. You're terrible too.

We may not remember all of the teachers, coaches, or other authority figures that we've had during our lives, but I am almost certain we all distinctly remember a few. Those people who connected with us by exposing us to a new concept or idea that broadened our perspective and resonated as true. The person who influenced our thinking so greatly as to set us down a path of curiosity of not only wanting to learn more but also perhaps to teach or convince others as well. It may not have been a single moment, but over time they said or did enough that our heart and mind were pricked, and we started on a long-term journey that resulted in a hobby, a career, or maybe even a passionate mission.

My guess is that there is a teacher who influenced you who just popped up in your mind.

This is why parents are so concerned with the quality of their kids' teachers, coaches, and other adult influences. We know the impact these people can make on our highly impressionable children, because we know the impact that particular people had on us. But often the people who influence us the most are not people who are in formal positions. Especially for high school and college students, those with the most influence are often our peers.

Obviously, peer influence can be good or bad. We all know the stories of (or have experienced personally) the teenager who started hanging out with a rough crowd who exposed them to ideas (or substances) that were harmful. Peers influence our body image, what we feel we must do to be accepted, and what we should desire or pursue.

Often during our teens and into our twenties, we get exposed to people outside our circle who have different ideas or philosophies than we have heard before. They may challenge our worldview and bring into question things that we believe. Sometimes we reject these ideas, but sometimes we feel as if our eyes have been opened.

When I was a junior in high school, I was finally allowed to put a small television in my room. Suddenly I gained access to the incredible world of late-night television—well at least the part that I could access from the dog-eared antenna. I became a raging fan of *Saturday Night Live* and enjoyed Johnny Carson's opening monologue (the guests were usually boring), but I discovered that other than that, there wasn't much on after *The Late Show*.

Until one night, when I came upon a fairly low-quality production featuring a commentator who talked about economics, private enterprise, and the role of government. I was transfixed. I had never been exposed to those concepts and immediately wanted to understand more.

Now, you may be thinking that if I was passionate about macroeconomic theory at seventeen, I was the dorkiest kid on the planet. And you may be right. But that person planted the seed for something I have been passionate about my entire life.

Once someone forms a strong belief about something, it becomes difficult to dislodge. In fact, our confirmation bias leads us to continually seek information that reinforces our beliefs and discount or ignore information that contradicts them. Protecting our closely held beliefs is a psychological act of protecting our sanity.

If you want to see the power of beliefs to fuel passion in action, go to a political rally or protest. You'll see people screaming, waving signs, even engaging in acts of violence in support of philosophies that often don't even impact them personally. They believe so passionately in an idea, they expend incredible energy to be heard.

Not everyone is going to march through streets to demonstrate about something they believe in, but all of us have beliefs that guide us. And they usually start with someone who influenced us. Sometimes it is simply the ideas that they exposed us to that resonated, but often it is because that idea is connected with a unique experience.

Experiences

I have a colleague who related to me something that happened during his childhood. He was at the end of his eighth-grade basketball season and hadn't seen the floor during a game for a single minute the entire season. During the car ride home with his parents after yet another game sitting on the bench, he sat in the back seat crying. He complained about the coach, how unfair it was, and how he wished he could play.

After a few moments, his father finally responded.

"Son, I know one thing about your coach: He's going to play the boys who he thinks will help him win. Obviously, he doesn't think you are good enough to help him win, so you aren't going to play."

He continued, "Now I don't care if you play basketball or not, but if you are going to do it, then put in the work to be great. If you're not going to put in the work to be great, then don't do it at all."

That was a seminal moment in that boy's life. Incidentally, he went on to have an incredible high school career and then an incredible college career and was eventually inducted into the Illinois Basketball Hall of Fame. He did the work to become great.

As he relates the story though, what is telling is how vivid his memory is of what happened. It isn't just something his dad told him one time. He relives the disappointment of not playing, the frustration with his coach, the anger and sadness all coming out in his tears. It was an experience that impacted him.

Throughout his professional career, he has been passionate about mentoring people who are willing to put in the work to become great. And consequently, he has a short tolerance for those who won't put in great effort.

Going through something firsthand has a far greater impact than merely hearing about it from others. Someone can explain what a hurricane is, but until you see the devastation with your own eyes, you just don't understand it. Experiences activate our senses and emotions to put us in a mindset to be open to new ideas in ways that nothing else can.

One of the questions I like to ask when I am interviewing someone is "Tell me about the best boss you ever had." Almost always, the answer involves a manager from early in that person's career.

Entering the workforce for the first time is stressful. You don't know how to do the job. You don't know how to act or even how to dress. You're not sure what to say in meetings or even how to get to the conference room that the meeting is in. And you don't know anyone you can ask. You are insecure, uncertain, and in a highly impressionable state.

I have a vivid memory from my very first professional job out of college when I went into my first meeting with our team. The VP of the division was there (which I didn't understand at the time was a rare and special occurrence) and he addressed the group about things going on in the business. In the middle of his remarks, he looked at me and asked if I was going to write down what he was saying.

I stared back at him blankly as I had nothing to write with or on. He of course could see that.

"Always bring a pen and notepad to meetings. Don't ever show up empty-handed again."

I was mortified, but I never forgot that lesson or that experience.

The answers I hear in interviews about great bosses generally go something like this:

> "I was just starting out and he taught me how to do this business. He taught me the skills I still use today."

> "She sponsored me and gave me opportunities to grow. She showed me how to thrive as a female executive."

> "He showed me how to balance being a successful professional and a good father. I have tried to model myself after him."

A few years ago, I was meeting with some of the younger, newer people in our company. I had asked the group to tell me something that surprised them during their first few weeks working in our business. One of the younger people in the group spoke up:

"Actually, it was more like a disappointment, and I guess a surprise. I had an idea of something we could try, and I went to the vice president who runs our team. He told me the idea was tried fifteen years ago and that it won't work. I mean, maybe things have changed in fifteen years? He totally shot me down and we didn't even really talk about it."

Forget for a moment all the potential business lessons in that story. Let's focus instead on the vice president. The idea he was shooting down was one that he himself had tried fifteen years earlier and had failed miserably. It was a professional embarrassment to him and left some scars. It embedded a firm belief that the idea was something that didn't work, and just the mention of it brought forth emotion. It would be really hard to dissuade him of that belief.

Since they are somewhat rare during a lifetime, big events get our attention, and sometimes we realize how impactful the event is even during the moment.

As a teenager, I had the opportunity to spend a month in Russia shortly after the Soviet government fell. For most of the people I met, I was the first American they had ever seen. I felt like a celebrity many of the places I went as people wanted to see and talk to me. But what struck me the most was the eyes of the people I met. The legacy of the Soviet government was one of oppression, and for seventy years they sowed distrust and suspicion among people. There was no path for improving one's life, merely a quest to avoid doing or saying something that would earn a trip to the gulag. The result of this environment was a malaise and hopelessness that I had never seen before. You could see the emotional shields in the eyes of the older people. Some were obviously afraid to talk to me or be seen near me. On the contrary, the young people I met had this amazing excitement for the future now that a new government was taking over. They were energetic and peppered me with questions about life in America. Many asked me if they could go back with me.

I was so overwhelmed by what I saw that even while I was there, I knew it would impact me for the rest of my life. Immediately upon returning, I felt this passion for the people of Russia and wanted to do what I could to help them. That zeal faded over time, but as I reflect now, I realize how much that experience informed my belief in freedom and individual worth—values I am still passionate about.

More common are experiences that we don't realize until later are impacting us the way they are. You hear this from people who leave unhealthy relationships: "I just didn't realize what an impact he was having on my self-esteem." Or bad jobs: "I didn't realize how stressed I was until I quit."

But often, our memory of experiences actually emphasizes the good over the bad. We tend to remember good emotions longer than negative ones.[1] You see this often when people have children and try to recreate the experiences of their childhood.

How often have you heard people say things like this:

"The way we grew up was so much better. We weren't stuck on devices all day—we played outside. Kids today aren't developing social skills—we played with the other kids in the neighborhood and figured things out. Kids are so sedentary—we stayed on our bikes until the streetlights came on."

Now, I'm not saying none of those statements are true, but they reflect an idealistic view of childhood that ignores so many of the problems we experienced (and by the way, our parents said the same things about us). We remember all the great parts of our own past and forget the problems, conflict, and hurt. Yet we use the beliefs generated by those memories to create rules and environments for our children.

It is invaluable to recognize how much our current view of our past experiences shapes our beliefs and fuels our passion for shaping our current world.

But none of our experiences create as much passion, for good or bad, as tragedy.

Tragedy

Viktor Frankl said, "We can discover this meaning in life in three different ways: by doing a deed, by experiencing a value, and by suffering."[2]

I have good friends whose young child was diagnosed with a pediatric brain tumor and given a few months to live. This type of tumor is so rare that there are virtually no treatments—there are so few children diagnosed with it that research is difficult. And sadly, there simply aren't enough people impacted for drug companies to be able to generate a profit from a treatment, so they don't allocate resources to it.

Their small family did everything they could to care for the child. They talked to doctors around the country looking for someone who could offer hope, but the best they found was treatment that could slightly improve quality of life. So they decided to shift their focus and enjoy the little time they had left together. Both parents took extended leaves from work, canceled virtually all of their social and community commitments, and just stayed together. When the child died, it was heartbreaking.

A parent losing a child must be one of the hardest possible things to go through in life. For many people, it is a blow from which they never recover. Seeing suffering in someone you love so deeply and have committed your life to protecting and then losing them creates an incomparable pain.

My friends' reflection on the experience was on how disheartening it is to go through something that is so rare that not only are there no treatments, but also there is no hope for treatments. As they mourned, they decided to make it their focus to create funding and research infrastructure on pediatric brain tumors and other rare diseases. This wonderful couple founded a charitable foundation[3] to help make the research possible that could lead to breakthroughs in treating rare diseases. They are passionate about creating hope and connection for other families who are going through what their family went through. Prior to this tragic experience, neither had ever even thought about medical research. Now it is all they think about.

This is a sad but common story. Tragic events in our life stir such great emotion that they make huge imprints. Tragedies can seemingly change what we care about and perhaps even what we believe in. Traumatic experiences can force us to rethink closely held beliefs and reshape the way we see the world. They can certainly change what we perceive as meaningful and joyful.

Receiving a cancer diagnosis is one of the scariest prospects most people could face. While the efficacy of cancer treatments has improved greatly, and many more people survive cancer today than in the past, there is still a risk not only of death, but also of deleterious long-term effects for those who survive. And the treatment itself can be incredibly difficult to endure.

In 2018, a study was done to compare the well-being of long-term cancer survivors with that of U.S. residents overall, patients who had recently been diagnosed with cancer, and individuals with chronic illness. The study's authors posit, "Because long-term cancer survivors face the risk of second primary malignancies and may live with complications from treatment toxicities, one might expect that they would experience a low quality of life."[4]

However, it turned out that the opposite is true.

That same study found this: "Although patients with cancer experience diminished well-being in the short term across a variety of measures, in the long term, cancer survivors do as well as or better than U.S. residents of similar age and demographic characteristics."

In fact, long-term cancer survivors scored significantly better than people nationally on well-being measures such as health, utility, happiness, employment earnings, and even health expenditures. That's right, despite the potential medical vulnerabilities caused by cancer treatments, long-term cancer survivors spend less on healthcare than their cohorts.[5]

Why is this? Author and Harvard professor Arthur Brooks suggests this:

> I have heard this story over and over: People don't realize their unhealthy attachments in life until they suffer a loss or illness that makes the important things come into focus. . . . Talk to them and they will tell you that they no longer bother with the stupid attachments that used to weigh them down, whether possessions, or worries about money, or unproductive relationships. The threat of losing their lives prematurely took a jackhammer to the jade encasing their true selves—the why of their lives.[6]

Being exposed to great pain and suffering of others can be just as impactful as when tragedies happen to us.

At the age of twenty-four, Janine Maxwell founded what would become one of the most successful marketing companies in Canada. For sixteen years, her company counted some of the most well-known companies in North America as clients.

On September 11, 2001, Janine found herself a part of the thousands of people trying to flee New York City. This event sent Janine on a search for the meaning of life. But it wasn't the fright of 9/11 that created a new passion. Her journeys took her to Africa, where she encountered the AIDS pandemic, hunger, and disease. Her heart was stirred by the faces of children, mothers, and grandmothers fighting daily for their lives.

Seeing these suffering people changed Janine. She decided to leave the business world and be a voice sounding an alarm for those too weak to cry for help. Ultimately, Janine and her husband, Ian, co-founded Heart for Africa, a faith-based organization that cares for hundreds of orphaned children in Eswatini.

Passion is going to fuel the choices you make in life. The things you feel strongly about and that stir your emotions can create a seemingly endless source of energy. The people and experiences that have generated the core values and beliefs about which you are passionate are going to determine what decisions you make in your life. If you want to be purposeful about your choices as you pursue a joy-filled life, it is important to be aware of where your passions come from and whether the actions that result from them are the ones you will be glad of.

CHAPTER 8

About Strength

"I DON'T UNDERSTAND WHY you would want this job."

The young man sitting across the table had just confidently answered my interview questions regarding his qualifications for the job. He was an internal candidate—someone who was currently a top individual contributor but was now applying for a management position. I had known him for years. Hearing my statement, he stared at me with a quizzical look.

"I don't understand what you mean."

I responded, "Let me ask you a question: What do you enjoy most about your current job?"

"Well," he said, "I love being able to figure things out and solve problems. I love controlling my destiny—I mean, I like that whether I succeed or fail is entirely up to me, because I know that I will figure it out. There's nothing better than the feeling of setting a goal for yourself and achieving it."

"Great. Now let me ask you a different question: What are the parts of the job you tolerate? Meaning you do them because you have to, but you don't enjoy them or they even frustrate you."

"That's easy—I really hate meetings. I mean, they are such a waste of time. No actual work gets done; we just sit around and talk."

"Makes sense. Anything else come to mind that bothers you in your current job?"

"I guess something else that bothers me is when other people don't get things done on time. Or when they don't take pride in their work and do a shoddy job. I mean, I depend on them so I can do my job, and when they don't deliver then I have to pick up the slack. I just wish they had some pride. Sometimes I wish I could just do my own thing and not have to depend on other people. Life would be a lot easier."

I paused for a second to let him calm down as he had started to get a little worked up.

"Okay, let me tell you what I've heard. You really like to be the master of your own destiny. You want the responsibility to deliver and the reward for doing it, because you know when it's up to you it will get done. You don't like your success to be dependent on others; you'd rather be in control. You don't enjoy having to spend time communicating and coordinating with others, because you can get things done more effectively if you just work on your own. That sound about right?"

He thought for only an instant before saying, "Yeah, that's right."

"Great. So I'll say it again—I don't understand why you would want a management job. Here's the thing, a manager's job involves doing everything you hate and leaves behind everything you enjoy. Managers work almost exclusively through others. Their success isn't determined by their own efforts but relies entirely on the performance of others. So they are constantly communicating with others as they coach, train, and support them. Oh, and they have to sit in a lot of meetings.

"Now, based on what you've told me, and what I already know about you, it seems to me that you would be miserable in a managerial role."

This time he took a beat before finally saying, "Yeah, you're right. I hadn't thought about it that way, but I guess I knew that."

"Then why are you applying for a job you know you'll hate?"

He paused and looked out the window for a moment before replying, "Because it's next. I mean, I'm supposed to advance in my career, right? That's what people do. And I'm pretty much at the top of what I can do as an individual producer. The only thing I can do to keep advancing is to move into management. So I guess that's what I should do."

I responded by telling him how much I liked and respected him, and that I hoped he would continue working there and achieving great things for years to come. Then I told him there were two reasons why I was not going to allow his boss to give him this management job.

I said, "First, it is my job to make sure that everyone here has a great manager who is highly invested in their success. That means their boss needs to love being a manager—they love helping other people succeed and want to be in that role for a long time. I can't put someone in a management role who doesn't feel a calling to lead and serve others.

"Second, and just as importantly, I care about you too much to do this to you. It would be incredibly cruel of me to knowingly put you into a position where I know you'd be miserable. Instead of doing that, let's focus on what you really want to get out of your career—not what you think others believe you should do, but what you really enjoy and are really good at. Let's figure out a way that you can achieve your goals in a way that helps the company too."

This time, he looked back at me with tears in his eyes. "I have to say, that sounds really good. Thank you."

This is not a fictional story. It is my best recollection of a real conversation that occurred a few years ago. In fact, it is only one of several times that I have had very similar conversations.

One of the great problems that arises out of not having a clear understanding of your own personal purpose, is that there is a tendency to replace it with what you believe your purpose *should* be. As we have stated, every action has a purpose—a desired result. When you are faced with a decision and don't know what result you want, you use your interpretation of what your parents/friends/boss/church/society believes your purpose should be.

I should try for the promotion. I should get married. I should be on social media.

Wait, who exactly said you should? Do they even know you?

The man in this story didn't have a clear understanding of what he wanted for his life, so he substituted what he thought he should want. He probably lacked the understanding of what a manager's role actually is, but his primary problem was a lack of self-awareness. He intuitively understood what he liked or disliked and what he was good at or not good at—he could easily answer the questions when I asked him what he liked and disliked about his current job. But he wasn't applying that knowledge to the decisions he was making in his life.

College

The senior year of high school is generally a lot of fun, but it also is pretty stressful. The way our education system works, seventeen- and eighteen-year-olds are faced with big decisions about their future: Should I go to college? If so, where should I go and what should I study? If not, what kind of job should I get? Should I learn a trade? Most people I know in their forties and fifties are still trying to figure out what they want to do with their lives; it seems naïve to expect teenagers with very limited information about the world to be able to decide.

Forty percent of undergraduate college students drop out before completing their degree.[1] Seventy-three percent of those (24.1 percent of total students) drop out in the first twelve months. At two-year institutions, an incredible 39 percent of students drop out during the first year.[2]

Having taken some college courses does increase career earnings, with college dropouts making an average of 18 percent more than those with just high school degrees (about $5,600 per year).[3] However, considering that college dropouts have an average student debt of $13,929.65,[4] it isn't clear if the financial tradeoff is a good one. Some 74 percent of college dropouts say they regret using student debt, so evidently, they don't think it was such a good deal.

Making the wrong decision about going to college can be an expensive one that creates challenges for years to come. So why do so many students who go to college drop out?

While many factors can cause students to drop out of college (social reasons, family demands, health issues), most surveys show that the top reason is financial. The primary driver of this is simply not wanting to borrow more money. Ostensibly, these students don't see the return they will get from school in exchange for the increasing debt. But given that people who hold bachelor's degrees earn nearly 50 percent more than those who drop out of college ($16,000 per year), it seems that more students would see those numbers and push through. What else is happening?

A study in 2022 asked students what their reasons were for not returning to school that fall. Two reasons tied for the most common: "Taking advantage of the current labor market" and "Not sure what I want to study." Twenty-eight percent cited their poor academic performance, and 24 percent simply said, "Higher education isn't for me."

Think about that—as many as three out of ten kids who go to college ultimately quit when, for some reason or another, they figure out that college isn't for them. In exchange for figuring that out *after* enrolling in college instead of *before*, they are saddled with debt that will take them years to repay.

I am convinced that many students go to college because they think they should—it is the done thing. Like the man I interviewed, they are just enrolling in college because it's expected—it's what's next. Maybe they see their friends going or feel pressure from their parents or teachers. Many may feel like they would be letting people down if they didn't at least try college. These kids are in the unfortunate situation of having to make important decisions when they don't understand themselves and their strengths, talents, and abilities enough to know what to choose.

An entire industry has been created to help students understand themselves and figure out what kind of jobs they may be interested in. There are numerous career assessments, guidance counselors, internships, and exposure programs for students trying to figure out what they should do. The experts understand that if students can align their studies for a career that will allow them to use their unique talents, then they will be much likelier to succeed and enjoy their studies and their jobs.

Unfortunately, many people don't get much more insight into themselves even as they age.

Executive Coaching

Executive coaches can serve as excellent guides for people who are going through or anticipating a transition in their career. They can work with someone who is trying to get a promotion, attempting to move to a new type of career, or who may have started having problems in their job performance and is trying to figure out how to fix them.

Virtually every executive coach begins their work with a client by giving them a series of assessments designed to help them get a better understanding of themselves. These assessments explore personality traits, interpersonal styles, values, and what they want from life. They also look for so-called strengths and weaknesses—things they are naturally good at versus skills that don't come naturally to them or that they haven't developed at all.

Carolyn Facteau has coached executives for more than twenty years, ranging from people early in their careers all the way to senior executives running businesses. For the past few years, Carolyn has also worked with executive MBA students. After having been in the workforce for a few years, these students have come back to school to learn new skills so they can move into a different type of career or advance in their current one. She starts by taking these professionals through her assessments. In my interview with her, Carolyn told me:

> For the vast majority of these students, being exposed to this information about themselves is an absolute epiphany that they didn't realize they needed to have. I regularly hear from the students that they came back to school because "I wanted to learn finance or accounting, but what I got the most from was all the time I spent reflecting on who I am and what I want and what I stand for. And then designing what's next for me based on that framework versus I'm in this track and this is the next logical thing. I thought I needed to go learn finance so I could run the finance department. Well maybe that's not going to bring me a lot of joy and fulfillment."
>
> Unless you have an experience like that or have an executive coach who focuses on that, people go their entire careers doing what's just logically next. And then being disappointed because they top out or they aren't very happy in what they are doing anyway.[5]

Carolyn compares this with the senior executives she coaches: "I have leaders whom I coach, and I ask them, 'Do you like leading people? Is this what you really want to do?' They go into leadership and they're not very good at it. They ask me to come in and coach them and really the fundamental problem is that they just don't enjoy leading."

This dynamic plays out in all kinds of roles, not just leadership. I have seen people who are highly social go into careers that involve sitting alone in front of a computer all day. They are miserable, look for any excuse they can to go talk to other people, and then struggle with performance because they aren't getting their work done.

Just like the high school counselor trying to help the senior figure out what to do after high school, good executive coaches try to not just help someone develop the skills they need for a certain job, but also help them understand themselves enough to know if that is a job that they are inherently suited for. In other words, do the requirements of that job match up with their natural strengths and tendencies? If there is not a match, then not only will the individual most likely struggle to perform well in the role, but they are also highly likely to be dissatisfied.

Understanding yourself doesn't just help you get a more fulfilling job but can impact every part of your life. Premarital counselors often start their work with engaged couples by administering personality and other assessments. The counselors realize that the more you know about yourself, the better you can understand what you truly desire in a relationship as well as your tendencies and expectations that will impact how you relate. So often when marriages fail, one or both of the partners express something along the lines of "We were young when we got married and I just didn't know myself yet. It turns out, we wanted different things."

I remember a statement from someone who had just gone through some deep self-examination exercises who said, "It was like looking in the mirror for the first time."

Mirrors don't lie; they reflect precisely what is. However, our perceptions of what the mirror shows can still deceive us.

Perceptions

We each have assumptions about ourselves—things we believe to be true—that act as a filter for the information we pay attention to about ourselves. Confirmation bias is just as relevant to how I see myself as it is to how I see the rest of the world.

I am an on-time person. I think it is disrespectful to be late. It is really frustrating to me when my partner makes us late. He is just not as organized as me and needs to plan ahead better. Occasionally, yes, I may cause us to be late, but there is always a good reason when I do it.

Nah, I bet you've never thought anything like that.

Part of seeking to understand your strengths is realizing what you aren't strong at, what you really have to work at or haven't developed at all, and understanding if the things you consider to be strengths actually are. It's seeing what is really in the mirror. Or more importantly, seeing how others perceive you.

A little while back I saw a picture and noticed someone in the background. It took me a moment to realize that it was me because I could only see my profile. I didn't see my usual view of myself—front on in the mirror while brushing my teeth or shaving.

"Whoa," I said to my wife, "when did my hair get so gray?"

"Uh, babe, it's been that way for a while."

"I look at myself every day and it's never looked like that!"

Not only can I not see myself from a side angle, but in my mind I also have an image of what I look like that causes me to not perceive the slight changes over time. It took seeing myself from someone else's viewpoint to get a realistic picture of what I actually look like.

There is a debate in personal development circles about whether it is more important for someone to focus on growing their strengths or improving their weaknesses. On one side, the argument is that doing things that utilize your strengths will cause you to get the results you desire—you rarely achieve great things or accomplish big goals by doing things you aren't good at. Conversely, being weak in some areas can result in behaviors that derail your ability to achieve your goals; and strengths, when they are overused, can also lead to derailing behaviors. For instance, if a leader who is naturally decisive but not naturally empathetic just decides to ignore his lack of empathy and double down on making decisions, he is likely to disregard the needs of the people he leads and run them off by making all their decisions for them.

I don't find the question of whether one should focus on building strengths or developing weaknesses especially useful. It forces an unnecessary dichotomy. Using and developing your natural strengths will not only help you get better results, but also more likely put you in positions of doing things you enjoy. However, if you aren't able to develop skills that aren't natural to you, then you are equally unlikely to succeed—or to enjoy what you are doing.

The more important and relevant question is this: How do I really understand what my strengths are—not merely as I perceive them to be or what I want them to be, but as they actually are?

Of course, we are also often our own worst critics. We see the blemishes in the mirror that no one else notices. We know when we could have done something better even though it appears fine to everyone else. Seeking to understand ourselves isn't an exercise in self-loathing. "Well, I used to think I was a pretty good friend, but I guess I'm terrible and everyone hates me." On the contrary, the more we understand about our strengths, the more we can respect ourselves and see our opportunities to improve as just that: opportunities. What a gift it is to have the self-awareness to be able to choose to focus my energy and strength in ways that bring the most joy into my life and the lives of others!

As my self-understanding gets deeper and more real, I am in a better and better position to make purposeful choices. What, then, are the ways I should think about myself?

If you ever have the opportunity to work with a coach like Carolyn and experience some of the many assessments on the market, I highly encourage you to do so. In chapter 11, I am going to suggest some questions and exercises to help you discover some on your own. But before we leave this topic, let's quickly lay out some of the different dynamics of ourselves that we should consider.

Physical Strength

I'm a decent swimmer. Back in my triathlon days, it was typically the event where I had better times. It takes a lot of training to build the speed and endurance to swim that kind of distance quickly, and so I put in a pretty good amount of time in the pool and my confidence grew.

Until one day when a friend of mine decided to "show and go" at a triathlon I was competing in. "Show and go" is a term triathletes use to describe people who do no training and then just show up to race. The unique thing about this lady is that she used to be a top-level collegiate swimmer who competed internationally but hadn't been in a pool in years. I was glad to see her on race morning, but a little worried for her safety since she hadn't trained.

What I didn't consider was that she is a physical freak. Not only did she smoke me on the swim, but she also had the fastest swim time of any female athlete and was in the top ten swim times overall.

Uh, guess I'm not as good a swimmer as I thought.

You just can't compete with genetics. Top athletes have musculoskeletal strength that lesser athletes simply can't top. I don't care how hard you work, if you are six foot one and LeBron James backs you down in the paint, he's going to win.

Physical strength may fade over time, but we still shouldn't underestimate the impact our physical attributes have on what we enjoy and are good at. The fact that we aren't world class athletes doesn't mean that our level of strength doesn't still fuel things we enjoy. I may not be as good a swimmer as my friend (who, by the way, I beat in the bike and run), but I still enjoy swimming laps in the pool.

And we shouldn't limit our thinking on physical strengths to athletic endeavors. Many people have great ears for discerning music, voices that lend to effective communication, or a physical "presence" that gets people's attention and commands respect. All of these attributes influence what they enjoy and help them get results.

Mental Strength

"How did you figure that out so quickly?"

Have you ever been around someone who can quickly do complex math equations in their head? Before you can even open the calculator app on your phone, they've already given you the answer.

Like physical strength, the raw horsepower of people with high intelligence is just innate. And being able to use that intellect in life can be both valuable and enjoyable.

However, mental strength isn't merely about IQ. Some people are blessed with an incredible ability to focus that helps them accomplish tasks in difficult environments. Other people have an innate curiosity that helps them quickly understand new concepts and apply principles across different disciplines. One key mental strength is what is referred to as a "growth mindset"—a core belief that, despite setbacks, you will continue to grow and improve over time.

Some types of mental strength allow people to be good at things that from the outside appear daunting or frightening. People who are calm under pressure can make excellent first responders or soldiers. People who are comfortable in tight spaces may enjoy things like deep water welding that frighten most people. Understanding attributes like these about yourself can help you choose situations where you can use them to your advantage and thrive.

Emotional Strength

EQ has become more commonly referenced over the past several years. Emotional Quotient leverages the more commonly known concept of Intelligence Quotient (IQ) to help measure a person's ability to manage their emotions, to positively impact their own mental state and their relationships, and to effectively interact with others.

High EQ is associated with the ability to recognize how your emotions affect yourself and others, to be real about what you are feeling, and to control impulsive behaviors that your emotions may cause. People with high EQ are highly empathetic—meaning they are in tune with the needs, concerns, and emotions of other people and pick up on the subtle cues that people give as to how they are feeling. They are excellent at fostering relationships with people; and as a result they can inspire and influence others, communicate effectively, and help resolve conflict.

Just like exercise can help you develop physical strength, emotional strength isn't merely genetic—you can improve it. And to function in relationships and society in general, everyone needs to achieve some capability to manage their emotions. However, some people are just wired in a way that these things come more naturally to them.

I once had a trusted colleague who was highly emotionally intuitive. She just picked up on things people did that everyone else seemed to miss. It was nice for me when she would come and listen to me talk about things I was dealing with, but she was incredibly helpful in pointing out others who could use help.

"Hey, I get the sense that John is struggling. You may want to check in with him."

I trusted her, so I went to talk to John. Turns out he was struggling. And engaging with him when we did not only helped him but also probably saved his relationships with his co-workers and possibly his job.

Whatever your strengths, being consciously aware of them will enable you to make choices that will lead to better results and more joy. Specifically, they often allow you to say no to things that won't allow you to do what you're good at and thus avoid frustration. Resist the temptation to generalize your strengths—"I'm a people person." Continually dig deeper by analyzing how you get results and what brings you energy. And be honest with yourself about what you think you are good at versus how good you actually are. The more accurately you see the reflection in the mirror, the better decisions you can make.

CHAPTER 9

About Legacy

A FEW YEARS AGO, my great-aunt (my father's aunt) sent him a picture she had found in an old album. The picture was taken in 1905. The feature of the picture is a man and a woman sitting in front of a tree. In the background are two kids who appear to be playing around a horse-drawn buggy.

I learned that those people are my great-great-grandparents. One of the children in the background was my dad's grandfather, my great-grandfather.

The people in the picture, my ancestors, were bootleggers. Most likely, the wagon in the background was used to carry illegal alcohol to their customers. During Prohibition, their son, my great-grandfather, became a moonshiner as well as a bootlegger. He didn't just distribute the illegal booze, he also distilled it. Great example of vertical integration. That's probably where I get my business sense.

My father told me about when he was a child and he visited the farm in North Georgia where this picture was most likely taken. His visit would have been in the late 1950s or early '60s. He distinctly remembers going deep in the woods to see the illegal stills.

It probably isn't shocking to learn that people whose livelihood comes through breaking the law don't make great life decisions. They placed no value on education, and my grandmother, for instance, only finished the sixth grade. It's no wonder that generations of bad decisions culminated in the environment my father grew up in that forced him into child protective services.

I also want to tell you about another person who lived on a farm during the same time in East Texas. This farmer had five daughters, who, while they were wonderful, he knew would have no future in farming. So he accomplished something practically unheard of during that time. Though they were poor, he worked hard enough so that his daughters didn't have to drop out of high school to work, but instead all five of his daughters graduated high school and eventually college.

After high school, one of his daughters got a two-year degree so she could become a teacher. However, she saw in her classroom that some students didn't learn the way others did and generally had to drop out, and others had no educational option at all. She married very young (as was common during that time) and made the highly unusual decision as a married adult woman to go back and finish a college degree. Using this degree, she applied for a grant from the county, wherein she was able to obtain use of an old bus barn where she launched the first special education program in East Texas that would accept Black students.

She became such a believer in the importance of education and spoke about it so often that all of her kids just understood that they were expected to go to college. But like her parents, she and her husband continued to work hard so that they could help them pay for it. When they graduated, she told her kids that it was now their duty to work hard enough so that they could send their kids to college. Her oldest son became a dentist, who sent four kids through college and then made them promise the same thing. His oldest, my wife, is keeping that promise right now.

It is true that eventually we will be forgotten and that those for whom we paved the way won't remember we existed. But that doesn't mean we don't impact others, both during our life and after it.

Our Impact on Others

The decisions we make and actions we take can only be measured by how they impact others. Those actions ripple out to those around us. Some of those ripples impact others immediately and some take much more time.

I love to hike. There is something about the rhythm of walking and the quiet solitude that is hypnotic and frees my mind to think. I enjoy hiking on remote, forested mountain trails where I rarely come across other people. These are usually very narrow, sometimes difficult-to-discern paths designed for one person at a time. When you do come across someone else, there is an inevitable semi-awkward interaction.

If they are going the other way, it's all about who can slide off the trail enough so that the other person can get by with their giant backpack. Usually, you have the obligatory "good morning" or "have a great day." Sometimes there are brief conversations about weather or questions about how far it is to the next landmark.

The more awkward interactions are when you come up on a slower hiker. First, you have to get their attention in a non-rude way so that they will slide over to let you by. But you also have to consider that, unless they are *really* slow, you are going to be walking near them for a while. So what do you do? Do you talk? Do you ignore them? Make fun of how slowly they walk?

Many years ago, I was meeting several friends for a weekend backpacking trip in a remote mountain area. Not all of us could get there at the same time, so we determined in advance where we would camp the first night so everyone knew where to meet. Those of us who got there first volunteered to get the fire going and start cooking dinner so it would be ready when the others arrived.

All was going splendidly until we noticed that it was starting to get dark and one of our friends still hadn't arrived. He was a very experienced backpacker during college, but over the last few years he had put on a lot of weight and gotten out of shape. It finally got dark enough that we began to worry, so I set off down the trail to see if I could find him. After hiking a couple of miles and calling out his name with no response, I came to a side trail that led to a shelter. I decided to hike down to the shelter to see if anyone camped there had seen my friend.

As I approached the shelter, still calling out my friend's name, I finally heard a response.

"Over here!"

I walked up to find my friend in his sleeping bag laying in the shelter.

"What are you doing here?"

It turned out that he had indeed struggled with the hike. And as it began to get dark he panicked and decided to just lay down next to the trail. As he told me the story, he pointed to another man and said:

"This guy came along and saw me. He took my pack and led me to this shelter for the night."

"Well, that's great," I said, "but why don't you come back to camp with me? We've got hot food waiting for you and everyone's there hanging out by the fire. I can carry your pack."

After some more convincing, my friend finally got out of his sleeping bag, repacked his backpack, and slowly followed me to the camp. We had a great weekend.

What has stuck with me about that experience is the guy who came upon my friend sitting next to the trail. He didn't have to help him. In fact, it turned out that he had expended quite an effort as he had to go drop his own pack at the shelter and then come back for my friend. It was really a nice thing he did for him. He had a choice as to what to do in that moment and he chose something that was hard for him, but good for my friend.

As we travel down the trail of life, we come alongside many other people. And in every one of those interactions, we get a choice as to what impact we will have. We can pass them by and ignore them, we can rudely bump them off the trail, we can walk with them for a while and encourage them, or we can stop and help them. Sometimes we will feel the impact we have in that moment, but often we'll never see where all our ripples go. I'm sure the stranger who helped my friend felt some justified satisfaction in assisting someone in need, but I bet he never dreamed that what he did would inspire me enough to write about it twenty years later.

I think of legacy as simply the impact that we have on other people—the imprint that we leave on others so that someone can know we existed. As we contemplate what decisions we want to make in our lives, it is vitally important to consider the legacy we desire. What impact do we want to have on the people in our lives? On the people in the future we haven't met yet or may never know? When someone describes the imprint we made on their life, what do we want them to say?

Impacting My Future Self

As we consider those people in the future that will be impacted by our decisions and actions, one of the people we need to keep in mind is . . . ourselves. The future me who is going to be impacted by the decisions I am making today. What are my actions doing to him or her? What kind of environment are we putting him in? What advantages are we giving her? What challenges are we leaving?

One of the questions I try to ask myself when facing a decision is, "What will I wish I had done ten years from now?" This question is powerful in helping me gain a perspective of the long-term impact of my decision. It helps mitigate my tendency to overweight a desire for short-term gains that will cause long-term regrets. It forces me to consider the impact that the decision will have on other stakeholders over a period of time.

But it also makes me consider a very important person—me. Not the version of me who right now is faced with a hard decision—or maybe one that just feels hard because it appeals to my desire for pleasure or comfort. It makes me consider the future me that is going to have to live with the repercussions of whatever decision I make.

All of us have done things that were exciting, fun, or pleasurable in the moment that caused problems later in our life. I wish that I was better at slowing myself down to ask myself this wise question all the time. The reality is that often the decisions I most regret are the ones that I make in an instant. Generally, when I take the time to step back and consider a decision and its long-ranging impact on all stakeholders (including the future me), I tend to make fewer decisions that I regret.

One discipline I have tried to develop is to realize when I am *reacting* instead of *responding*. In my lexicon, reactions are in the moment, instinctual actions that are caused by some outside stimulus. You insult me and I react by insulting you.

Responses involve a pause between the stimulus and my action. You insult me and I wait for a moment to consider my action.

That pause is important. It allows us to consider all the things that drive our decisions—our emotions, our desire for pleasure, our beliefs, our values, and, hopefully, what we really want out of life and how this action is going to impact us. The more impactful the decision on me and others, and the more emotion I feel around it, the longer of a pause I probably need.

This is why we (hopefully) take time to make big life decisions. We seek advice, we make lists of pros and cons, and we consider alternatives. We don't want to rush into a job, relationship, or purchase that we will regret. It's also why when we see someone else making a big decision very quickly, we worry for them.

"Whoa. I hope he doesn't regret rushing into that relationship."

Unfortunately, we don't always have the luxury of time to make decisions that could have long-lasting consequences. Often, we are faced with crises or pressures that require us to respond in the moment.

This is one major reason I believe it is so important to have a conscious, articulated understanding of your values, beliefs, and desired legacy. When you are faced with having to make a split-second decision and don't have clarity of your desired experience of life, you will default to your subconscious drivers—things like security, comfort, and pleasure.

One of my personal goals is to train my reactions to look more and more like my responses. I want to have so much clarity about how I want to experience life and the legacy I leave, that even the decisions I must make in a split second are the ones that my future self will be glad I made.

When we think about legacy—the impact we are having on others—it is important that we consider that impact from the other person's perspective and not merely our own. Often, we think we are doing something good for someone else, but don't consider the damage we are actually causing.

In many cases, this mismatch leads to regret. I have had multiple conversations with retired men who talked about how hard they worked when their kids were young. "I wanted them to have the things I never had and teach them the value of hard work. What I didn't realize was that they just felt neglected and now they want little to do with me."

But in many cases, we never see the damage we are doing. Sometimes our best intentions can lead to problems for others, but because we never take the time to consider their perspective, we don't realize it.

Sometimes, even our actions that have the best of intentions can be harmful to others. The philanthropic world is full of stories of charities that did more harm than good. They gave money or service to people in need, but by doing so created dependency or hurt those in the community who were trying to earn a living by providing that service. The rich people who gave the money felt good about giving money to help those in need, but never realized that in the long run their gift actually hurt the people they wanted to help.

I want to close this chapter with a story. I love this story because it forces us to consider the real legacy we are going to have on others, not a fantasy that we are telling ourselves.

The Parable of the Engineer

There was a boy who grew up in a beautiful but remote part of Northern California. His home was on what wasn't actually, but for all practicality was, an island. On one side was a river and on the other was the cliff of a great mountain. The only way off the "island" was via a rickety old bridge that went into the small town nearby. Every day his family and the few others who lived on their little island traversed this bridge to go to work, to school, or to shop for the things they needed. Each time they wondered if today was the day that the bridge would fall; always knowing that if a flood came, they would be trapped.

These daily trips on the bridge made quite an imprint on the boy. He would spend hours looking at that old bridge, trying to figure out how it stood. Over time he discovered that he had gained a passion for engineering. Much to his parents' pride, he applied and was accepted into the state's top engineering school. Upon graduation, he immediately went to work as a structural engineer. Word of his ingenuity and creativity quickly spread in what was then still a small community of engineers, and he was recruited by the country's top engineering firms. He eventually became known as the nation's great bridge builder—designing colossal bridges that crossed some of the mightiest rivers and ravines in the country.

After many years of building bridges and as he approached the end of a successful career, he learned that he was sick and was given only a few years to live. He decided that he wanted to spend his remaining time back in his home on his little California river island. When he returned, he saw to his surprise that little had changed in the intervening years. The town was still small, and people still crossed that rickety bridge that by some miracle was still standing.

The engineer decided that he wanted to give his community something that he was uniquely able to give—a wonderful, beautiful bridge. So he went to work. He used his influence and marshaled the small town to get behind the effort. He helped them understand what investing in a structure like a bridge could do for the community. He told of how he had seen so many small towns that were transformed into growing, thriving cities once they were able to have people and goods flow freely. "Investing in infrastructure is the path to a prosperous future," he told them.

Convinced, the town poured everything they had into funding the bridge. And the engineer designed a masterpiece. Not only would it be sturdy, but it would be beautiful as well. It would not only be a conduit for great commerce but also something that travelers would go out of their way to see. And being attracted to the bridge, surely they would be attracted to the community and desire to live in such a place.

His design was so beautiful, in fact, that he decided to move the bridge to the other side of the island so that it could be seen more clearly as vehicles approached on the state highway. "If we are going to get the full impact of a structure such as this," he said, "we must allow it to be seen in all its glory." So convinced of its worth, the engineer poured all his personal wealth into its construction, making up for the final funds unable to be borrowed by the town from the few banks that would lend to such a poor community. He may die penniless, but he would go assured that his money went for something worthwhile.

As the engineer became more ill, the bridge was finally completed. Though he was now confined to a wheelchair, he came out to a grand-opening ceremony for which not only the whole town turned out, but also officials from neighboring cities and even the governor, who all came to see this feat of engineering and art. And what a work it was. Crowds meandered across the bridge, but mostly gathered at the entrance to see the magnificent statues of the black bear—the very symbol of California.

Speeches went on for hours about the changes that were coming to the town. And it was all thanks to the engineer. On it went as dignitary after dignitary spoke of his great gift to the town. To his delight, a bronze plaque that had been placed on the entrance of the bridge was read aloud to the crowd. In this plaque engraved with eloquent prose, the town dedicated the bridge with enduring gratitude to the engineer.

Satisfied that his life's work was complete and that he had achieved something that would indeed be a lasting legacy, the engineer died three days after the ceremony.

For the first few days after its opening, the bridge was very busy as townsfolk wanted to utilize the bridge of which they were so proud. And indeed, travelers on the state highway would slow down as they passed the bridge so they could see the beautiful statues that adorned its entrance.

But after some time, the traffic started to lessen, and shortly there seemed to be fewer and fewer people using the bridge. And in a matter of just a few weeks, it seemed that eventually no one used the bridge at all.

And all the growth that was to come to the community? Well, it never happened. And without the tax revenues from all the expected growth, the town had to use all its money just to make payments on the debt it had incurred to build the bridge. Nearly bankrupt, the city had no money to maintain the bridge, and it quickly began to fall into disrepair.

Many years later, a man was traveling down the state highway with his family. As he approached the bridge, he didn't just slow to take it in, but actually stopped so that he could see it more closely.

And what he saw frightened him. This man was an inspector with the state and his job was to ensure that bridges and roadways in California were safe. What he saw before him was anything but safe.

Despite being on the way to a vacation with his family, his professional duty overcame him, and he drove into town and found the city hall. He stormed in and, utilizing his state credentials, demanded an immediate audience with the mayor.

"I have just come from inspecting your bridge," he said. "It is in terrible disrepair and is unfit for pedestrians much less vehicles. I am shocked that you haven't already had a terrible catastrophe."

"No need to worry," the mayor assured him. "No one uses that bridge. No one ever really has."

"I don't understand. It obviously cost a great deal. Why build a bridge such as that that no one would use?"

The mayor replied, "Well, it was before my time, but I think the problem is that the bridge didn't go to town. It was built on that end of the island so that people could see it, but it didn't go anywhere that people needed to go. There is an older bridge on this end of the island that we have recently reinforced, and it works perfectly well. So there is no reason to use that old bridge and, as far as I can tell, there never has been."

The inspector was amazed at the story but undeterred in his desire to clarify what he knew needed to happen. "Well, if there is no reason to repair it, then the town must tear it down."

"Oh," the mayor replied, "we have no funds to do that. This is a poor town. For years nearly the entire budget went into paying the debt on the bridge, and we had no money to invest in anything else. Businesses left and the town almost ceased to exist."

"Something must happen," the inspector pressed. "That bridge is owned by the town, not the state. If it were on the state highway then state funds could be used. But since it is on the town's property, the town must do it. You have six months to demolish the bridge or the town could be fined."

As the inspector left town on his vacation, the mayor gathered some of the town leaders to determine what to do. With no money, they certainly couldn't afford to tear down the bridge. What were they to do?

Six months later, the inspector came back to town. But this trip was no happenstance—he was now on official duty to ensure that the bridge had been destroyed. As he drove up the state highway, he began to grow concerned as he could see the entrance to the bridge ahead. He groaned as he began to mentally prepare himself for the inevitable confrontation with the mayor as he told him of the fines that would be levied on the town. However, as he got closer, he saw something strange. The entrance to the bridge was untouched, but the middle had disappeared. A fence had been placed across the entrance so that one couldn't fall off the end. While unorthodox, he had to admit that the townspeople had indeed found a way to uphold the spirit of his directive if not the letter. After a further inspection, he decided that he would approve this remedy and not bother the town further.

As he was leaving, he noticed that there had been some bushes recently cleared away from the base of one of the great statues at the bridge entrance. Curious as to why someone would take the time to clear this area as they were doing the minimum necessary to rectify the danger, he walked over to take a look. And then he saw something he had never noticed before—a great bronze plaque. Despite the years of aging, he could just make out the beautiful inscription that ended with a dedication to the engineer.

But below those weathered words, there was a crude, yet obviously recent addition to the engraving. With amazement he read the words aloud.

"His hubris burdened us all."

Having reflected on the three major areas that impact the way we uniquely think about our life—our passions, strength, and desired legacy—we are now ready to more closely examine our self and articulate what we want from life. In the next section, we will walk through concepts that lead to specific, personal questions that will help us create clarity about our purpose.

Get ready, this is when the real work starts.

PART 4:

EXAMINATION

"Up ahead they's a thousan' lives we might live,
but when it comes it'll on'y be one."

—John Steinbeck, *The Grapes of Wrath*

CHAPTER 10

About Seasons

I LOVED PLAYING SPORTS as a kid. I played football in the fall, basketball during the winter, and baseball in the spring. I hung sports paraphernalia all around my bedroom, including a huge poster of Michael Jordan on the ceiling. I was destined for sports greatness.

Or maybe not.

As I aged and reached the limit of my playing ability, that passion evolved from playing sports to following sports. As a young adult, I would watch college football all day Saturday and NFL all day Sunday. One year I watched more than a hundred Atlanta Braves games in their entirety. I regularly read the whole sports page and all the articles in sports magazines. I knew every stat and was deadly in a game of sports trivia.

Watching multiple football games in a day became a little more challenging after we had kids, but I learned to prioritize and still get in the important ones, especially including my home state Georgia Bulldogs.

One late Saturday afternoon, I was sitting in my favorite chair watching a Georgia game (no memory of who they were playing) as my wife and very young kids had dinner at our kitchen table just behind me. Not surprisingly, someone on our team did something stupid and I started yelling at the TV (because that always makes your team play better).

Just then, my four-year-old daughter stood up from the table, walked up beside me, and put her little hand on my arm.

"Daddy, are you okay?"

It was that moment when I lost my passion for following college and professional sports.

As soon as I felt her touch, I realized that I had literally turned my back on my family during a meal to let a bunch of eighteen- to twenty-two-year-old boys I didn't even know steal my attention and control my emotions. I barely watched a game for the next decade—I was just much more interested in my family.

Over the next few years, I developed a passion for coaching youth sports. I had the opportunity to coach all my kids on various teams and even got to coach my daughter on a highly competitive travel team all the way through high school. The joy I got from working with those young athletes, watching them struggle and put in the effort to overcome, was better than anything I could ever get from playing the game. As much as I still love to compete, during that season of my life I was just much more passionate about coaching.

The Search for Passion

As your age and the circumstances around you change, what moves you does as well. What stirred your heart when you were in your twenties and single is different than when you are in your thirties with young kids or your fifties as an empty nester. But changes in interests or passions are not just related to physical changes or your family.

As we experience new things, the novelty of those experiences that creates such intense emotions wears off. The first time seeing the ocean can be an amazing, even overwhelming experience. The hundredth time you see it is just another day. The passion aroused the first time you go on a date with your future spouse is very different from how you feel when you celebrate your twenty-fifth anniversary. Even the professional accomplishments that energized you early in your career aren't as enticing later in your career.

Ask any business professional who is over the age of thirty how they feel about business travel. You will most likely get an answer on the scale between "I tolerate it" to "I despise it." But if you ask them how they felt when they were in their twenties and got to go on their first business trip, they'll probably tell you it was exhilarating. They loved getting to stay in hotels, eat at nice restaurants, and fly in airplanes. Remember when you first got frequent flier status and got into the airline club with the free watered-down drinks? That was so cool!

Closing the big deal, cashing the big check, going on the incredible trip, getting the promotion, gaining the recognition. Over time the allure changes. Sure, it's nice that your boss thinks you can take more responsibility, but understanding the strain and stress that will bring may not sound as great as it once did.

Our hearts and minds grow numb to things we have already experienced. The thrill we feel from something we've never seen or done before becomes harder to replicate. As we realize that the things we desired early in life didn't bring the satisfaction or lasting results we hoped for, a real melancholy can set in. Paradoxically, the more you get to experience and achieve in life, the worse this problem becomes. Many people reach middle age and feel like they just can't get passionate about anything anymore. They have "checked so many things off the list" that it's hard to find anything to get excited about. Like developing a resistance to medication, their emotions don't react to the things that they used to.

I don't want to skip past this lightly. Feeling an inability to experience passion is a common and serious psychological challenge, and for some it's something they never get past. Having experienced this personally and walked alongside others who have also, I have found it is helpful to start with the realization that passions will change over time. It isn't just you—it's a natural and potentially even wonderful part of life. Understanding that passions change with seasons allows you to release the passions of the past instead of clinging to something that is fading in its ability to bring enjoyment. It also allows you to embrace a new set of passions that can bring the same or even greater satisfaction than the old ones. Passion is out there, and you can find it again. Like Janine Maxwell, who went on a global search for meaning after 9/11, you simply need to search for it. And the even better news is that the search itself can be exhilarating.

Not as Good as I Once Was

One of the depressing things about being a runner is the inevitable decline of speed. For years, I would track every mile as I worked through training plans designed to make me faster. Year after year I would set personal records at various distances, and it was so rewarding to see my hard work pay off.

Until I got old. And then no matter how hard I trained, my running pace just kept getting slower and slower. And worse, the harder I trained the more often I got injured and then I couldn't train at all. As a triathlete friend of mine once told me, "Getting old sucks. I don't recommend you do it."

When my kids were young, I would be up at 5:00 to train, in the office by 7:30, home at 6:00 for dinner, put the kids down at 8:00, and then back on my computer working until 10:00. Every day. I was building a business and loving every minute of it. I would take a short nap on Sunday afternoon, but otherwise

I seemed to have energy that didn't quit. It was a really fun and rewarding part of life.

I still love my job and work hard at it, but on days when I get up at 5:00, I'm exhausted by the afternoon. And when I try to work late at night, I often notice the next day that the emails I sent the night before are full of grammatical errors and barely make any sense.

Did I mention getting old sucks?

Except that there are some things that I seemed to have actually gotten better at with age. It turns out that I am way better at my job now than I was twenty years ago. I know where to focus and how to quickly identify and solve most problems that appear. I am much better at evaluating talent and have surrounded myself with an incredible group of colleagues who are so good at what they do that they make my job much easier. Having better learned what I'm good at and what I'm not, I have created a team that leverages their expertise in my weak areas so I can focus on where I uniquely create value. This makes me more effective and leaves me more time to seek areas to add more value to the business and do things I enjoy. It's pretty great.

And I am much better at mentoring and coaching others. I have simply seen so much in our business and in my career that I have a good sense of what people are going through. I've improved my listening and empathy skills and can provide better guidance for the people who work in our business, and often outside of it as well.

Now, this might sound like I am going on a rather long-winded speech of boasting about myself, but this description of myself isn't unique. In fact, I'm describing the evolution that most people go through. When we are young, we have the energy to brute force solutions to problems and achievement. As we age, we naturally lose some of that energy, and the creativity and drive that goes alongside it. However, what replaces it is great depths of understanding and insight.

In his wonderful book *From Strength to Strength*, Arthur Brooks describes these two phases as *fluid intelligence* and *crystallized intelligence*.[1] Fluid intelligence is raw smarts—the ability to reason, think flexibly, and solve novel problems. Crystallized intelligence is the ability to use a stock of knowledge learned in the past. In other words, you develop vast amounts of wisdom.

My personal definition of wisdom is *the discernment to know the best methods to achieve the best objectives*. In other words, it takes wisdom to know both what you should pursue and how to get there.

During the first half of your career, you leverage your energy-fueled fluid intelligence to creatively solve problems. Because you haven't seen the problems before, you are able to approach them in novel ways—occasionally in ways no one else has. This time of life is the source of great innovation and invention and is paired with the energy to put in the hard work to pursue it.

During the second half of life, you have the benefit of all the dumb things you tried and failed at when you were young. You don't have to keep relearning old lessons. Further, you can apply all those lessons to new settings so that you can make better decisions faster. And though you may not have the energy to pursue every great opportunity, you have the ability to guide others that do.

Brooks calls the fluid intelligence period the first intelligence curve and the crystallized period the second curve. The good news for us is that as the first curve starts to decline, the second curve is growing.

One application of understanding these curves is that the two groups really need each other. Those with high fluid intelligence need the older people to advise them so they don't waste energy chasing ideas that will never work. Those with high crystallized intelligence need some young people around to keep their mind open to fresh ideas and keep up with changing environments. It's a different way of thinking about diversity on a team.

Understanding that our strengths can change over time is both liberating and empowering. It can be very depressing to continually judge ourselves by standards that measure areas of declining strength. When I look at my running pace now compared to ten years ago, I get really down.

But knowing that I haven't simply gotten weaker but have simultaneously gotten stronger in other areas allows me to focus on activities that utilize the things I am good at. I now know that I don't need to do a ten-mile run with negative splits to feel good. Running four miles and maintaining a steady pace actually makes me feel just as good and keeps me healthier.

Unfortunately, our Western culture largely glorifies youth and emphasizes the negative aspects of getting older. You don't see any facial creams at the drugstore designed to make you look older. But continuing to focus on activities that leverage old strengths is not only futile but also unnecessary. Continual awareness of how our strengths are changing allows us to choose activities that are both more effective and more enjoyable.

Changing Impact

My oldest two children are only seventeen months apart in age and they have a younger brother who trails them by a few years. One of their favorite pastimes is to complain about the different standards applied to their younger sibling than were enforced on them.

"Are you kidding? We never would have been allowed to do that! What happened to you guys? Who are you? How are you letting him get away with it?"

On and on it goes.

"When we were young we always had to . . . we never got to . . . you never would have . . ."

To which my favorite response is:

"Guys, here's what you have to understand—we just love him a lot more than we love you."

That always gets a fun reaction.

Okay, okay. Let's all come clean. Every parent will admit that the standards might change a teeny tiny bit between the first child and last child. I mean after all, parenting lasts for a long time and eventually we just get tired of all the effort.

But that's not quite the whole story.

My wife and I were at dinner in a restaurant a few weeks ago and were seated next to a young couple who had brought their very young child with them. We immediately knew that this was the couple's first baby. We could tell because they were constantly cleaning every single item the child could possibly touch. Every surface was covered with plastic. The baby wasn't sitting in the booster chair per se, but in a completely sanitized seat cushion that was placed on the restaurant's booster chair. Every time the toy or binky was dropped to the floor, the mother would pick it up and wipe it down with a sanitizing wipe before handing it back to the child.

"Wow, do you remember when we were that way with our oldest?"

"Yeah, by the time the youngest came along we basically just let him eat off the floor."

Changing standards for our kids isn't merely because as parents we get lazy, it's because our experiences tend to alter what we think is important. The lessons we want them to understand, the values we want to impart—while some of them are timeless, sometimes things that used to seem like a really big deal don't seem as big anymore. Or something that we used to consider non-negotiable is now more malleable.

As we go through different seasons of our life, the impact we desire to have on others and on our future self changes. Many of the decisions we made in our twenties that we thought were going to set us up for life now seem silly in retrospect. Our decisions now are based on the desire for a very different legacy. The principles we so badly wanted other people to agree with that we would passionately and loudly march through the streets chanting have been replaced by other beliefs that have been refined over time.

Understanding yourself—your passions, your strengths, and your legacy—isn't a one-time exercise. Articulating your purpose—what it means for you to experience your most joy-filled life—isn't something you do and then put in a frame never to be touched again. It's a journey. It's a continual refinement as we carefully consider all the additional terrible and wonderful experiences we endure. It's embracing the natural changes that occur in ourselves as we pass through the seasons of our life and allowing those changes to guide us into even more joyful actions and mindset.

I hope you embrace the process of exploration and articulation involved in clarifying purpose in your life. But I also hope you don't put the unreasonable pressure on yourself of getting it right for once and all time. The journey is too much fun to only experience once.

CHAPTER 11

About Your Mantra

A MANTRA IS A word or sound that is repeated often to aid in concentration. Originating as a Hindu and Buddhist concept, mantras were thought to have spiritual power. I wouldn't subscribe to that theory but can attest to the power of having a mantra that helps me focus on something important.

You may prefer to call it a mission, a vision, or a purpose. I like the idea of a mantra because it feels actionable. Whatever you want to call it, having a statement that is clear, unambiguous, and easily recalled is a powerful tool in bringing decisions to the conscious level to assure you are living purposely.

This is your opportunity to actually do a little work. You may be tempted to rush through this chapter and go on to the next section, but I encourage you to resist that temptation and instead take the time to dive in. Even if you have done some of this before, it will be worth doing it again with a fresh perspective. At a minimum, I suggest you read through the exercises and consider what they are trying to bring out. By the end of this chapter, you are going to have a mantra through which you will be able to filter the many decisions of your life. It's worth doing.

Exercises

As we have said, the ultimate question you are trying to answer to determine your purpose is, "How do I experience the most joyful version of my life?" The way you get there is by deciding how to make the innumerable choices that you face. Specifically, you must decide how you want to spend your time and energy in a way that gives you the most joy. The answer to that is your chosen purpose.

It would make no sense to say that you want to craft a purpose that results in you doing things that you aren't passionate about. Conversely, if you can make choices that regularly connect you with things you are passionate about, you will have no problem making those decisions and following through.

Here are some exercises that I have found helpful in understanding what I am passionate about. To do them properly, you really should use a pen and paper. I would suggest you use a notebook or journal that you can keep and reference in the future. I like to redo these periodically to contemplate what has changed.

Lifeline

Start on the left side of the following diagram and draw a solid line that ends on the right side. The left end represents your birth, and as you go across the page you are getting older, finally ending at where you are today. Going up and down represents the highs and lows of your life. Think about and write in the events that were happening during that time that caused the line to be high or low. Here is an example:

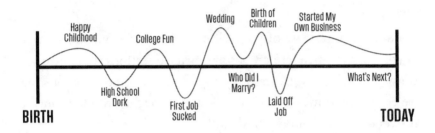

Stories

Write out the story of some events that have occurred during your life. The first category of stories should be about moments that gave you great joy—where you felt whole, complete, satisfied, or loved. The second category should be stories about moments of great sadness—times you felt loss, shame, defeat, or loneliness. You should have at least one story for each category, but if you take time to really reflect, you probably have more.

These may correspond with the major events you identified in your Lifeline but will also probably include experiences that didn't rise to that level. Maybe the story is something that didn't seem like that big of a deal at the time, but as you look back you think, "Wow, I was really happy then." Or maybe it wasn't something that greatly changed your life but made you sad at the time.

It is important that you actually write the narrative of what occurred. Pretend you are writing this so that someone who doesn't know you could fully understand what happened. Give the context, describe the people involved, and explain the emotions you felt while it was going on. Perhaps even explain how the event impacted you later. Writing the story will help you relive it and help accomplish the purpose of this exercise—raising your awareness of things that created or stirred your passions.

Interview Yourself

Conduct an interview of yourself and then write out the answers to your questions. Here are a few starter questions, but since you know yourself so well, you may also think of some questions that are especially powerful for you. Again, don't just think about the answers—write them out in detail!

- What breaks your heart?
- What gets you really excited?
- What makes you angry?
- If you could plan the perfect day, what would you do? Who would be there?
- Describe a day where you would have a hard time getting out of bed.
- What's the most valuable thing you learned from your parents? Your best boss? Your worst boss?

Rule Book

This is an exercise I have used with business teams for years, but it can be even more powerful for an individual. The goal is to write down a rule book for your life. You are not creating new rules, but identifying the rules that you already live by. The following are the beginning of sentences. Finish them with as many answers as you can think of.

- I believe I should never . . .

- Every day, I should . . .

- A mistake I will never make again is . . .

- When it comes to money, I . . .

- Something I consider unforgivable is . . .

Strengths

Let's spend some time identifying what you are really good at. Think through and write out answers to the following:

- Some things that come easily to me but seem to be difficult to others include . . .

- Things that others ask my opinion about or ask for my help with are . . .

- The parts of my job that I really enjoy are . . . . The parts I just tolerate are . . .

- If you asked your spouse / significant other / best friend what you do that strengthens your relationship, what would they say? What would they say you do that harms the relationship?

- Pretend you are a scout who is evaluating your fitness for physical activity. Where would they rate you highly?

Exploring Seasons

Let's move on to a new exercise. Write out the answers to the following questions.

- What is something you used to spend a lot of time doing but don't do anymore? Why?

- What is something you used to argue about but don't care much about anymore?

- If you had a free afternoon with absolutely no commitments and nothing needed from you, what would you choose to do? What would you have done ten years ago?

Leaving a Legacy

Think through these scenarios and explain your desire for what will happen.

- A group of people has gathered to create a plaque that will be placed in your honor. Who are the people in the group? Where will they place the plaque? What will it say?

- You have hired a coach to help you in personal development. She starts by interviewing some key people in your life—family, friends, and colleagues. The first question she asks them is "How has s/he impacted you?" Who does she talk to and how does each of them answer?

- Toward the end of your life, a famous author decides to write a biography of your life. He spends a lot of time researching you and then you sit down with him for an interview. He asks you, "As you look back, what are the things that you are most glad you did?" and then, "What are the things you did that you most regret?"

- It's your funeral and the time comes for the eulogy. The person speaking walks up to the podium and looks out at the crowd. Who is the speaker? Who do they see in the audience? What do they say?

Putting It Together

Read back through all that you have written and circle or highlight key words that you see. Look especially at words or phrases that appear often. Think through your identified strengths and how those impact the things you want to do in your life. Consider the legacy you want to leave to your future self and others.

- Write a list of some of these key words and phrases.

Now, experiment by combining them into various sentence structures. Consider starting the sentence with one of the following phrases:

- I exist to . . .
- My purpose is to . . .
- I will live so that . . .
- I will experience joy when I . . .

Keep experimenting until you get to a sentence that resonates with you and is short enough for you to easily remember. Anything longer than fifteen words is probably too much!

Don't feel like it must be eloquent or perfect. You will continue to evolve this over time and maybe even before you finish this book! Just make sure it is something you can remember and that you understand what it means. The goal is that when you are facing a decision, you can say this phrase to yourself to remind you of your purpose—what will give you joy—and it will help you decide what to do.

Congratulations! You've got a mantra! Now, let's talk about how we can use it.

CHAPTER 12

About Activation

GOING THROUGH INTENSE SELF-EXAMINATION is an emotional experience. Thinking about people who influenced you, tragedies that occurred in your life, how you are impacting those you love, how you will judge yourself at the end of your life, and how you will be remembered is hard and sometimes even painful. The strong emotions those thoughts create can be exhausting but can also create a tremendous sense of urgency. It is not uncommon for deep introspection to cause an awareness of desired changes—and even a near panic from wanting to make those changes quickly.

Perhaps as you went through the process of writing your purpose statement, some things you want to change in your life became immediately clear to you—something you need to start doing, something you need to resume doing, or something you need to quit doing. Perhaps you realized that you are in the wrong job, the wrong relationship, or spending time doing the wrong things. Maybe you put this book down after the last chapter and made some life changes before picking it back up to start reading again.

More likely, you realized that there are some areas where you want to change, but after stepping away for a moment you started to get a little overwhelmed as to where to start. I mean, it's great to have this idealistic view for how I can live a purposeful life, but I still have to make a living, take care of my kids, and pay my bills. I'd love to think I can just uproot my life and go change the world, but that's not realistic.

What can I actually do with all of this?

How much time do we have?

Another common reaction is an acute awareness of time. Thinking about your mortality and how you are spending your life today forces you to face the fact that your time is limited. Every day you waste doing something that doesn't bring joy is one that you will never get back. Considering all the responsibilities I have and how much of my time is already committed, how do I actually start weaving in activities that are more meaningful? I'm afraid I'm going to fall back into my normal routines when I really do want to make a change. I want to spend more time with my family. I want to spend time doing things I love. I want to be more aware and more present, but I have too much to do. How do I balance all of this?

I don't want to look back ten years from now and realize I wasted all this time!

If you have felt or thought those things or anything like them, you are in good company. You can use those emotions to create energy to move forward. And if there are obvious changes in your life you desire to make, then get to it. For the rest of us, it's hard to know where to start. And there is a big danger of never starting at all.

You have probably had "mountaintop experiences" before that caused great emotions and a deep desire to change. Perhaps it was at a retreat where you were exposed to great teaching of truth. Maybe it was at the birth of your child or after meeting the love of your life. You gained clarity about changes you needed to make in your life and were determined to make them happen. But then, when you got back into your normal environment, your old routine took hold, and the realities of life distracted you. The emotions that were so intense on the mountain started to fade and, before you know it, you were right back doing the things that you have always done.

Having experienced this kind of cycle may be feeding a fear about your inability to live in a purposeful way and wasting your valuable and perishing time. It may have even made you cynical about whether anything can ever really change. I mean, all this purpose stuff sounds nice, but real life takes over and I have to just get back into the grind. It's best not to even get my hopes up.

The journey of understanding your purpose is a long and difficult one, but learning how to activate your purpose—how to actually live in a purposeful way—is arguably even harder. Let's start by taking the pressure off.

Focus on the Journey

You are not going to make the leap to living a perfectly joyful purpose-driven life in one day. Wait, scratch that—you will never master living a perfectly joyful purpose-driven life. So don't make that your benchmark. Instead, remind yourself that learning your purpose and how to live it is a journey. The goal is to keep getting better at it—not master it. Simply take the next step. As you go, you will gradually improve. You will learn from what works and from your mistakes. You will refine your purpose some, but you will refine what you do with it a lot.

After writing your purpose statement, you may have been surprised that there were so many chapters left in this book. The reason is simple—knowing your purpose is pointless (maybe even painful) if you aren't equipped to do something with it. What comes next— learning how to activate your purpose—is arguably more important than what has come before.

I was made keenly aware of this a few years ago. I agreed to work with a small group of people to take them through some of the exercises in chapter 11 together. Each finished with a statement that they even read to each other. It was a powerful moment.

About three years later, I was in a discussion with several of the people from that original group and their purpose statements came up. Disappointingly, there were only two who could remember what they had written. The others talked about how they remembered it being meaningful at the time, but they never did anything with it. One said, "It kind of hurts to think that for the last three years I have never thought about doing anything around my purpose."

That conversation saddened me, but also caused me to push to see what was different about the people in the group who remembered their statements. Was it something inherent about them that made them more prone to think deeply or care about their impact on the world? I followed up and asked those two to talk about what they had done with their purpose statements to see if there was some common trait between them.

It turns out that those two weren't smarter or more caring and more concerned with their impact on the world. What made it stick for them seemed to be simply that they were more disciplined. Not disciplined in the "I get up early every morning to exercise and never eat carbs" kind of way. They had developed little reminders, mnemonic devices, and practices in their life that helped keep purpose top of mind.

I say disciplines, not habits, because as I stated earlier, the good things in life rarely become habitual but seem to always require discipline.

As I reflect on my own journey, I realize that as I began to get clarity of my purpose, I started looking for ways to activate that purpose and developed disciplines to help me follow through. It started small, but once I started seeing the results of purposeful living, I loved it and wanted more. I wanted to get better at living purposefully. I began to see more and more areas where I could apply purpose. And I began to experience joy in more and more areas of my life—even areas that were unpleasant.

This desire to get better at living purposefully is one of the commonalities I have noticed among people who have a clear sense of purpose in their lives. It is part of the never-ending journey of understanding and applying purpose.

Just like hikers need a map, compass, good shoes, food, and water if they are going to make it down the trail, those who start the journey of purposeful living need some tools. Otherwise, we can get lost, tired, and discouraged—and just turn around and quit.

Now that we are equipped with clarity around the purpose of our life and even a mantra to help us remember and apply it, we can shift our attention to how we can actually begin living it. But before we start making plans, in the next section we will consider some important realities that impact how we can live purposely and continually improve at it. We will start by exploring how anyone gets better at anything.

PART 5:

CONSIDERATION

"Muscles aching to work, minds aching to create—this is man."

—John Steinbeck, *The Grapes of Wrath*

CHAPTER 13

About Performance

HERE'S SOMETHING THAT EVERYONE already knows—youth sports have really changed over the past couple of decades. One of the most popular topics among middle-aged adults is comparing the way we played sports as children to the way it is done today.

If you are above the age of thirty, you've probably heard someone say something like this: "When I was a kid, I played four different sports. I would put the basketball down in the spring, pick up the baseball bat, and not touch a basketball again until the next winter. These kids today have to specialize at ten years old and they play the same sport all year round. This is ridiculous!"

As someone who has coached youth sports for several years, I have pretty strong views on the state of youth sports in America. Maybe someday I'll write a different book on that, but you will probably be able to guess some of my views after reading this chapter.

Years ago, I was coaching a team of middle-school girls who played competitive softball. We would travel around our area playing in tournaments against other top teams. We didn't have as busy of a schedule as many of the teams we were competing against, but it was still very demanding on these young girls. They had to go to practices each week as well as work with hitting, pitching, and catching instructors and do their strength workouts. When we played tournaments, these kids would be gone for entire weekends. Oh, and they also had to do schoolwork and their chores at home, and deal with hormone-crazed relationships with their friends. It's a lot.

One week at practice as we were preparing for a tournament, I could just tell that the girls were tired. It was late in the season and the school year, and they were just grinding down. So I told them that instead of having the next practice at the field, they were all going to a different park, and instead of wearing softball uniforms, they should wear normal workout clothes.

They all showed up with looks of dread on their faces, assuming that I was about to put them through a grueling strength workout to build stamina. I took them all out to a grassy area beneath some trees and sat them down.

"I want to tell you something that you probably don't know," I said. "Despite what you may have heard, you do not get stronger or faster from working out."

They stared at me with quizzical looks on their faces until one girl broke the silence by standing up and yelling, "Would you please tell my dad that because he is always making me work out!"

"Hold on!" I said. "Let me finish. You don't get stronger or faster from working out. You get stronger or faster by recovering from working out. You must have both. If you only work out and never recover, you don't get stronger, you just get hurt."

We proceeded to spend the next hour doing yoga and being quiet in the shade. Well, as quiet as teenage girls can be.

Recovery

Here is a concept you probably learned in your high school health class. When you exercise a muscle, the fibers break down. After rest, hydration, and nutrition, the fibers grow back together stronger than they were.

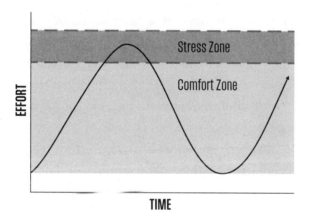

Athletes can comfortably keep up a certain amount of effort for a certain amount of time—their *comfort zone*. But as time or effort increases, they get beyond what they can comfortably do and they enter the *stress zone*. The stress zone is where things start breaking down. They can stay in the stress zone for a little while, but eventually need to go back into the comfort zone before they give out.

This period in the comfort zone following a time of stress is the *recovery period*. This is when the muscles get the opportunity to rest and rebuild.

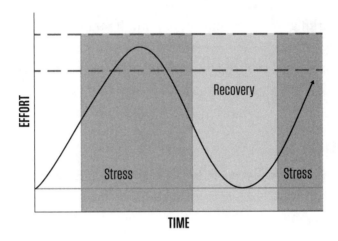

Some refer to this pattern of stress and recovery as the power cycle. As an athlete regularly stresses their muscles and allows them to recover, their comfort zone expands. What used to be difficult for the athlete now feels easy. A level of effort that they could only sustain for a little while can now be sustained for a longer period. And they are able to recover from periods of stress more quickly.

In theory, this basic principle of *stress and recovery* guides the training of every level of athlete. You stress your muscles and when they recover, they are stronger. Unfortunately, many novice athletes either don't understand or choose to ignore this principle—they just keep working muscles harder and harder until they break down. Worse, many coaches and parents directing kids neglect to apply the principle of stress and recovery.

Ask any sports medicine doctor and they will tell you one of the most common injuries they see in young athletes is from overuse. The athlete keeps using the same muscles over and over without rest until those muscles give out. When athletes show up with strained muscles from overuse, the treatment prescribed by the doctor is almost always "rest."

It is worth noting that the opposite problem is also true—and arguably much more common in society at large. One way to foul up the principle of stress and recovery is to never recover. The other way is to never stress. Lack of recovery can lead to injury. Lack of stress leads to atrophy—your muscles get weaker. Instead of an athlete expanding their comfort zone, the zone starts to contract. Things that used to be easy become hard.

Finding the right balance between stress and recovery is very difficult to discern for athletes. Knowing whether staying in the stress zone a little longer is going to help you get stronger or lead to injury is a fine line. Athletes are constantly told to "listen to your body," but figuring out if your tired body is telling you that you need to back off or is just naturally reacting to the stress zone is very difficult to discern.

Periodization

High-level athletes apply this philosophy of stress and recovery in multiple ways. I wasn't a high-level athlete, but during the years I did triathlons I learned a lot about how training plans are created. Endurance athletes (like most athletes) leverage a concept called *periodization*. This concept applies the philosophy of stress and recovery simultaneously across different time periods.

First, athletes think about how they will get stress and recovery each day. They have their daily workouts as well as specific plans about what kind of nutrition they will take in and especially how much and when they will sleep. In fact, many professional or world-class athletes get ten-plus hours of sleep each day including taking daily naps. They are simply putting so much stress on their bodies that they need a significant amount of time to recover through sleep.

The second period is weekly. Every day in a week is divided into stress days and recovery days. When I was training, I always had one day each week where I did no training at all—it was purely a recovery day. It always amazed me how much better I felt in my workouts on the day following a recovery day. But the workouts during the week also have varying degrees of difficulty. Even some workout days involve lighter workouts so that they serve as recovery days for the very difficult workout days.

The third period is monthly. My plans always included three "build weeks" followed by one "recovery week." Each week had six days of workouts, but recovery week workouts were a little lighter, shorter, or easier. Those were the weeks where the benefits of the training from the previous three weeks set in. Again, I was always amazed at how much better I felt in my workouts following a recovery week.

Finally, periodization is also applied annually. When I was racing, my year was divided into three seasons—"A" season, "B" season, and offseason.

"A" season was when I had my top races. These were the ones where I really wanted to perform well. For top racers, these may be qualifiers or national championships. My whole year was designed around "peaking" for those races—meaning I was at my absolute best condition of the year when I showed up on race day. For me, "A" season was the four months leading up to my biggest races, and the training during those months was the hardest I did all year.

"B" season came right before "A" season. The purpose of "B" season was to build a foundation of sport-specific fitness that would prepare me for the difficult workouts during "A" season. So the "B" season workouts, while challenging, were relatively easier than those in "A." I would do races toward the end of "B" season, but they weren't the ones where I really wanted to perform well. The purpose of those races was really to help me train on race-specific skills and measure my progress in training. "B" season also lasted about four months.

Then there was "off" season. The purpose of offseason was to let my body recover after eight months of grueling exercise and be sufficiently rested so that I could do that again the following year.

Now, offseason may sound like the four months of the year when I sat on the beach drinking margaritas. Relative to "A" and "B" season, offseason was certainly easier and less time consuming, but it involved doing completely different kinds of workouts from the rest of the year. Instead of spending each day on a bike, in the water, or on a run, I would do many other kinds of exercises designed to create muscular balance by strengthening the muscles that I didn't normally use. It also helped to break the mental monotony of doing the same thing over and over. For me, offseason involved a lot of things like lifting weights and doing yoga. And then drinking a margarita.

Stress and Recovery in Professional Sports

Scottie Parker has trained players in the NFL and the NBA. As a head trainer, his job is to make sure that some of the best athletes in the world become stronger, quicker, and more explosive. Further, he has to create a plan that enables them to maintain that conditioning over grueling seasons with high-pressure games and intense practices in between. And that's before the playoffs even start, when the schedule and intensity step up.

According to Parker, the importance of recovery in how he creates plans for the athletes "is massive."

"Recovery has a cumulative effect. Just like anything in your life that compounds—your money, your health, your training—the effect of recovery compounds. When you do something over and over, like lifting weight, the cumulative effect of the effort compounds to make you stronger. It works the same way with recovery."[1]

An athlete can improve their recovery skills just like any other skills. They can improve their ability to recover more fully and more quickly. However, this compounding effect can work for and against you. Parker explains:

"If an athlete doesn't put any emphasis on recovery until January (mid-way through the season), at that point they are too far behind. Two nights of great sleep and great hydration is not enough to pay the debt that they've accrued."

Parker also talks about how recovery plays out in different ways.

> People think just about how a player recovers from one game until the next one that is two days later. But you see this play out even inside games. Some of the best athletes are the best at recovering—they are able to quickly recover inside a game. The guys who are really ready to go—they might have a ten-second break in the game and have a heart rate of 180 and in ten seconds they can come down to 145. There is a micro-recovery. Another guy may only make it to 174 and then he starts again, and it spikes to 190.
>
> But that difference is going to point back to how well you trained and how well prepared you were for this event. And to see that preparation, you have to see how well you applied recovery principles over the course of the entire season.

Not surprisingly, Parker doesn't let his athletes off from the hard work required to develop world-class conditioning. The offseason involves four-week periods with three weeks of intense training followed by one week of recovery workouts. But all of those start after four to six weeks of total rest immediately after the season is over. He calls those weeks "a big de-load block."

> Their body has been so beaten up for seven months that they just need to let it regenerate. Go outside and go for a walk, but don't touch a basketball.

Manage–Don't Avoid–Stress

You have probably figured out by now where all of this is going. This concept of stress and recovery isn't limited to athletes or even physical performance. It is the only way that anyone ever gets better at anything.

No one improves without stress. Stress is the hard work. It's the effort you must put forth to get something done, learn a new concept, develop a skill, or improve mastery. If you want to be excellent at anything, to achieve high performance, or even maintain mental health, stress is a necessary ingredient.

It should go without saying but unfortunately can't: No one achieves anything worthwhile without working hard and expending great effort, without stressing themselves. The word *stress* has gotten a bad reputation, but it's an incredibly misunderstood concept. Saying that someone should avoid stress is basically saying that someone should avoid growing or improving at anything.

What should be avoided is continually enduring stress without time for recovery. Just like athletes who overuse a muscle by not resting it, when we don't allow ourselves to recover from the stress in our lives, we too will get hurt. Worse, we can hurt those around us.

We need healthy amounts of stress in our jobs if we are to get better at it. We need to put forth uncomfortable amounts of effort at times so we can improve our relationships. It is necessary for us to challenge ourselves to do hard things if we are to grow as an individual. But just like the athlete who can only run so fast for so long, we can only maintain those high levels of effort before we give out and fail our jobs, our relationships, or ourselves.

Just like athletes, we need to think about recovery across multiple time periods—daily, weekly, monthly, annually, and maybe even longer over the course of our life. And just like athletes, recovery doesn't simply mean lying on the couch and eating potato chips.

Recovery involves doing things that strengthen infrequently used muscles—exercising the parts of us that aren't used as much.

When the principle of stress and recovery is applied well in our lives, we can not only improve in the different areas of our life, but we can also improve our ability to recover from the hard things that come our way. In other words, we can handle more while building resiliency from the things that knock us down.

How do we think about and practically apply this concept of stress and recovery in our lives? What does it mean to exercise infrequently used muscles outside of athletics? How do we create periods of recovery throughout our day, week, or year?

Before we can answer those questions, it is important to first understand the different parts of our lives that we must consider.

CHAPTER 14

About the Elements of You

ONE SATURDAY MORNING EARLY in my triathlon career, I joined an organized group ride of cyclists in my area. This group rode the same route each week and would break into three groups based on the fitness and experience level of the riders.

Riding in a group of cyclists is thrilling. It's hard to explain what it feels like to experience the "draft" that occurs when you are riding in the middle of a lot of other riders. You don't work that hard, yet you're going really fast.

Group rides with new riders can be dangerous, as one miscue in the middle of a peloton—the main body of riders in a group ride or race—can cause a massive pileup and injure other riders. But riding with other cyclists is also one of the fastest ways for a new rider to learn about the sport. You get the opportunity to observe how more experienced cyclists ride, set up their bikes, or manage food and liquid intake. Most cyclists are incredibly friendly and love talking about their sport and helping new riders. And cyclists always love to talk about gear. What's the newest wheel or cassette? What size ring do you use for climbs? What kind of brakes or saddle? Gear talk can go for hours and on long group rides is a great source of conversation.

On that Saturday morning, I was a little nervous about being a new cyclist in a group ride and frankly just didn't want to screw up. After going for a few miles, I got the hang of it and the peloton spread out some so we were mostly riding side-by-side (versus in a big clump), which was a little less stressful and more conducive to conversation. Finally a little more relaxed, I started talking to the rider next to me and quickly learned that he was a very experienced cyclist and, like I hoped to be, a triathlete.

"What advice would you give me as a new triathlete?" I asked him, thinking I could get some insight into what kind of handlebars or gear setup to use.

"I've done triathlon for several years and here is what I've learned," he said. "Triathletes only have room in their life for three things—their job, their family, and triathlon. The problem is that you can only be good at two of them. So you have to choose which two."

At which point he accelerated ahead of me.

I have no idea who that guy was, and to my knowledge I have never seen him again. But that concept has stuck with me ever since.

Work, life, and what else?

The idea of work-life balance became popularized in the latter part of the twentieth century. During the 1980s, the women's liberation movement brought awareness of the work-life balance concept through the introduction of ideas like flexible working schedules and maternity leave as a way to accommodate more women in the workforce. The concept was quickly expanded beyond women, with the idea that everyone desires balance between their professional and personal lives.[1]

In the span of less than forty years, work-life balance went from a new concept to a primary driver of employment. A 2022 survey showed that 90 percent of workers said work-life balance is "an important aspect of their work."[2] In a second survey from the same year, 63 percent of job seekers said they prioritized work-life balance over better pay. Companies now compete for talent by advertising their focus on work-life balance—creating amenities, policies, and benefits that enable employees to more easily spend time on activities that don't involve their work.

Yet despite the desire for more work-life balance, Americans work roughly the same number of hours per year as they did fifty years ago.[3] This conflict between desire and reality has created a massive number of frustrated people trying to figure out how to achieve the mythical balance. In response, work-life balance has become a multimillion-dollar industry as numerous consultants, authors, and speakers attempt to help people solve this problem.

One of the challenges we face in figuring out work-life balance is trying to understand what is meant by "life." We get the work part—that's the place I go for forty hours a week (or log into from my home computer). But the life part, well, that encompasses a lot of other stuff—my family, friends, health, faith, community, hobbies, and so on. Which of those do I spend time on? When exactly am I supposed to do all of that?

And by the way, what if I really do need to work more than

forty hours a week because I need the money? What if I like my job? If I start a business that requires a lot of time, does that make me a bad person?

Several models have been created to help people understand the different parts of their life. Leaving behind the simplicity of categorizing everything either as "work" or "life," they include eight, twelve, fifteen, or more components. Each describes parts of our lives and is helpful in making us aware of important activities involved in living holistically.

Further, understanding the different parts of your life can help you be aware of your need to spend time and energy in each area and avoid the pitfalls of only focusing on one or a few and neglecting the rest. This is an important concept and one we will explore more deeply.

While I find these models helpful, the challenge for me lies in their complexity. My problem is that I can't remember fifteen different things, much less figure out how to do anything about them.

The Power of Three

A few years ago, I accepted an invitation to help a friend who was struggling in his business. He asked if I would facilitate a session with his senior leaders to come up with their strategic and operational plan for the following year. He was obviously frustrated with his team and wanted my help in getting them to execute.

"The market is changing, and our customers are demanding something different," he said. "I know what we need to do, but it just feels like we can't get anything done."

I gathered in a conference room with the team and started by asking them what their current plan was. My friend quickly projected onto the screen something titled "Annual Plan" that consisted of twelve objectives, each with target dates and achievement metrics. He commenced with reading through all of them, but after a few I stopped him.

"Do me a favor and turn off the projector."

He looked at me strangely, obviously a little mad that I had cut him off, but acquiesced and took the image off the screen.

"First, tell me, where did the twelve objectives come from?"

My friend replied, "We all met last year and came up with the key things we needed to do to become more competitive in the market. This was our list."

I suspected that while he was crediting the group, he was probably primarily responsible for the list himself, but I ignored that.

"So the group agrees that these are the twelve key objectives for the business for this year?"

Heads nodded.

"Okay, please tell me what they are."

People started reaching into briefcases to get their printed version of the plan, and my friend began to restart the projector.

"No wait. You can't look at the document. Just tell me what they are."

I went to the whiteboard and waited. Eventually, people started saying them, or at least rough approximations of a few of them. After a few minutes, we got to six and the chatter stalled.

"What about the other six?"

Someone started to say something, but a colleague pointed out that it was already on the list.

I looked at my friend for the answers and he stated two more before getting a blank look on his face.

"Okay, pull the screen back up."

We looked at the list and I heard a bunch of "Oh yeah" and "I forgot about that one" from the room.

"Next question: How many of these did we accomplish this year?"

The group looked sheepishly at each other until one of them sort of mumbled the answer: one.

"So you guys only accomplished one objective this year? How many did you make progress on?"

A little offended at being called out, they began arguing among themselves about things they had accomplished. After about ten minutes of this, I cut them off again.

"I'm going to give you credit for five. So, to be clear, last year this group got together and came up with a list of twelve key objectives that the business had to accomplish to become competitive in the market and survive. You made progress on five, accomplished one, and don't really remember the rest."

In my years of leading a business and having worked with leaders on hundreds of strategic and operational plans, one of the most consistent problems I've seen is when groups have too many goals. You can't focus on twelve things. Saying you are focused on twelve things really means that you aren't focused on anything.

Regardless of what you've heard, multitasking isn't a thing—you cannot focus on multiple things simultaneously. You can do an activity that accomplishes multiple purposes simultaneously (and I love to look for those highly effective activities!), but that is different.

When we do strategic planning, I insist that the leader or group agrees on no more than three priorities. I'm not sure why, but there seems to be power in the number three. It's hard to remember ten things, but we can easily remember three things. When my wife sends me to the grocery store and only needs three things, I have no problem. When the number of items goes beyond that, I have to start making a list.

Inevitably, groups start with a much longer list of important things to be done. I usually let them off the hook and tell them that they can keep the longer list around so that they know what to do next after finishing the first three, but they must decide which are the three most important. And even those three won't be equally weighted—at least not for everyone and not at the same time. This process can be incredibly difficult to do as there are so many things that businesses must do well to succeed.

The Power to Change

Call it a goal, objective, initiative, or whatever you'd like—organizations that are trying to improve, pivot, or merely survive all have things they are trying to change. Change, whether organizational or personal, requires focus, creativity, and energy.

Most of us learned about Isaac Newton's laws of motion in high school physics. Just in case you don't remember everything from that class, here is a little refresher about his first law: *A body remains at rest, or in motion at a constant speed in a straight line, unless acted upon by a force.* This law is summed up as the principle of inertia.

Inertia is a concept that applies to more than just moving objects. It is also very descriptive in understanding human nature. Organizations and individuals have ways of doing things (or not doing things) that become ingrained and comfortable. Once we get all the wheels in motion a certain way, they develop a momentum of their own. Causing them to do something differently requires the application of energy. To create change, you must battle inertia.

Inertia can work for us and against us. When we get used to doing things that are beneficial, they can become second nature and we no longer must devote energy to them. We simply make sure they keep going.

But change is different. It's hard. It requires application of focused time and energy. And those are the two truly limited elements in the universe.

One of the primary reasons I have seen people become disillusioned in their quest to live a purposeful life is that they are simply trying to do too many things at once. Fueled by passion to change their life, they attempt to do everything at once. They make it too complicated.

I often ask leaders to explain their strategy. Usually, I get a long-winded answer that is incomprehensible to me, and I suspect often to the leader as well. If they can't explain it to me, then I know that the people they lead don't understand it either. And if they don't understand it (or can't remember it), then they won't be able to act on it.

Making something simple is much harder than making something complicated. One of my favorite quotes is attributed to Mark Twain: "I didn't have time to write a short letter, so I wrote a long one instead."

One thing I have learned through leading dozens of businesses—to get organizational focus on executing a strategy, the strategy must be simple enough for everyone to understand. It may be a very complicated product or service, but it still must be boiled down in a way that people can easily understand so that they know how to act.

I have learned that this is also true for me as an individual. Thinking about the many facets of my life and trying to apply my purpose to everything is too much. I can't comprehend it, much less have the time and energy to handle it all at once.

Part of the wisdom the cyclist imparted on me so many years ago was an understanding that we must choose where we will put our focus. Choosing to focus on something means we are devoting time and energy to that thing. It also means that we are choosing to not spend our time and energy on something else. Since improving at something requires spending time and effort on it (time in the stress zone), you simply do not have enough time and energy to become excellent or even improve at multiple things at the same time. You must choose.

The other insight I gained from him was that we really can encapsulate our lives into three separate yet overlapping categories. In my experience, all the parts of my life, all the different things I do, the way that I spend my time and energy, fall into these buckets. The wonderful benefit of there being three is that I can remember them, so I can be consciously aware of them, and therefore I can act on them.

I have come to believe that our lives consist of three general elements—work, relationships, and self. We will explore each in the next three chapters.

CHAPTER 15

About Work

FOR THOUSANDS OF YEARS, our ancestors constantly needed to work to survive. Nearly every waking moment was dedicated to doing something necessary to survival—finding food, creating shelter, or avoiding danger. The story of human development consists of people doing work that made it easier for the species to survive. We worked to develop tools to help us find and cook food more easily. We worked to create more reliable kinds of shelter. Then to create more effective forms of transportation. And communication. The list goes on. This history of humans is a history of creating, innovating, and improving—of working. We are inherently wired to work—to create value and improve our environment.

Protecting Your People

Work isn't merely something we must do so that we can eat and have shelter. Humans are wired with the innate desire to not only procreate but also propagate—to make sure that we as a species survive and grow. This drive causes us to work to protect our progeny.

Ask almost anyone who has a child, and they will describe to you that when they first held their baby, they felt this surprising and overwhelming sensation to do whatever they could to protect that child. Even people who had carefree or even risk-seeking attitudes before parenthood will tell you how much they changed when realizing their responsibility of caring for a baby. Parents are consumed with protecting their children and work tirelessly to do so. We want to ensure our kids have what they need and aren't exposed to things that could harm them. I can't tell you how many times I have seen first-time parents come back to work after the birth of their child with a new level of seriousness about their job. They are no longer working just for themselves but for someone else.

For many, this drive goes well beyond working for the good of just their immediate family. I have the opportunity to regularly speak with CEOs of all kinds of organizations. Again and again, I hear in their voice the burden of responsibility they feel for the employees and the families that their organization supports. There is incredible satisfaction in being able to create something that provides for the needs of so many people. There is also significant pain when you are unable to protect it.

The spring and summer of 2020 was inarguably the most tumultuous moment of our lifetime. The societal and economic shutdowns played havoc on people and businesses. Every business leader experienced incredible uncertainty in trying to determine the right course of action as they attempted to navigate the most uncertain circumstances imaginable. And nearly every business was faced with the question as to whether they had to lay off employees.

In the depths of the lockdown, I sat with a friend who leads an incredibly successful business. We were sitting in my backyard (socially distanced of course) when he told me about the decision he had made that day to furlough and terminate thousands of employees.

"Everything we do involves getting people together in physical spaces," he told me. "Literally, we have shut down everything."

And then, with tears in his eyes, he said, "This company has been in existence for decades. I'm not going to let it go down on my watch. I won't stop working until every one of those people is able to come back to work."

And he didn't.

The pain in his voice wasn't driven by pride or an egotistical need to prove he could lead through adversity. It came from a much deeper need to protect his community.

Throughout human existence, people have expended great effort to create protection for themselves and those around them who they depend on. In ancient times, this was demonstrated by groups working together to create walls of defense around their village. Today, it involves people agreeing to set aside parts of their income (taxes) to pay for systems that provide clean water, education, and emergency services for their community.

I am fascinated by people who develop land and particularly those who specialize in creating infrastructure. For a few years, I served on the board of an organization that allocated some of our community's money that had been set aside for transportation projects. I was regularly exposed to engineers who conducted detailed analysis to predict what types of investments we needed to make to be able to support our community in the future. These dedicated people got incredible satisfaction out of the fact that their work would make it easier for those around them now and in the future to take care of themselves. They are continuing a line of work that stretches back to the beginning of human existence of altering the landscape to make it easier for people to survive and thrive.

Working Outside of Work

We often confuse our need to work with having a job. Indeed, many people solve their psychological need to work through their vocation, but people who don't have jobs still seek ways to contribute or create value. And many people who have jobs that they don't enjoy or don't find rewarding solve their psychological need to create through other activities unrelated to what they are getting paid for.

I had a friend years ago who, after years of working in a professional services job, decided that he wanted to rekindle his musical skills and write songs that he could sell. So, in addition to doing his job and being a father to his kids, he began dedicating huge chunks of time on nights and weekends to writing music. Certainly, he was passionate about music and loved doing it, but I sensed there was more going on than enjoying a new hobby.

One day, he asked me to help him work on a song he was composing. During a break, I asked him how he was able to keep doing his job with all the time he was spending composing. "You are up until 2:00 in the morning every night. Aren't you exhausted at work? How are you doing your job? Are you going to get fired?"

"My job is so easy, I could do it in my sleep," he said. "I'm just a cog in the wheel there. I don't even have to think. I just do what I need to do and then leave. I'm barely noticed."

I have seen this same dynamic in so many people. They are earning a paycheck working somewhere that they can barely tolerate while they are much more energized by work they are doing on the side—renovating their house, making items to sell online, writing a book, or engaging in politics. My friend wasn't composing music merely as a passionate hobby. He was doing it to satisfy his psychological need to create.

There has been much written in business media over the past few years about employee engagement. A quick online search can find article after article explaining that one of the main reasons people are not engaged or even dislike their job is that they don't feel like they are making a difference. Why is this? I would argue that when someone says they don't feel like they are making a difference, it means they aren't satisfying their inherent need to create something that is going to help those they care about. And if they can't satisfy that need through the place where they earn their paycheck, they will find some other way of doing it.

Early in the book, we talked about the natural human desire to seek comfort; a result of this desire is that we are wired to be lazy thanks to our body's efforts to conserve scarce resources. One upside of our natural drive to be lazy is that it causes us to look for and create ways of being able to be lazier in the future. In other words, we are naturally inclined to create new innovations that will enable us to be more efficient—we will do extra work now so that we can do less work in the future.

One day when I was in college, I came back to my dorm room and noticed that there was this long pole lying next to my roommate's bed. It consisted of several small sticks that had been taped together with a rectangular piece of plastic at the end. It had obviously taken a lot of time to make, and I couldn't figure out why in the world my roommate had spent the time to create it.

"What in the world is that?" I asked my roommate who was lying on his bed reading.

"Ah man, check this out! I like to have the lights on when I'm reading, but then when I'm tired and want to go to sleep, I have to get up and go across the room to turn off the light switch. So I created this."

He proceeded to pick up his ridiculously long pole and carefully guide it to the light switch and somehow managed to push the switch down.

"Great, huh?"

We will work really hard to be lazy.

It is in our very nature to work to provide for and protect ourselves and those we depend on physically and emotionally. And because we know how hard it is to survive and thrive, we instinctively try to do things that will make it easier for us and our loved ones. Regardless of our level of wealth and comfort, when we deny or ignore that instinct, we create problems for ourselves.

The Myth of Retirement

The entire concept of retiring—of removing yourself from work and becoming solely a consumer versus a producer—didn't even exist until about 150 years ago. That means that for 99.9 percent of human existence, the thought that someone could stop working at some point in their life never crossed anyone's mind.

To begin with, for much of human history, relatively few people lived long enough to reach a point where they were physically unable to work. It is generally agreed that life expectancy in the pre-modern world was around thirty.[1] Throughout most of human history, infant mortality has been around 25 percent (meaning one-quarter of children didn't survive the first year), and only around 60 percent of people lived through puberty (meaning four out of ten children didn't live past age fifteen).[2] Adolescent children just faced so many challenges to survival—disease being chief among them.

If you could make it past the age of fifteen, then there was a decent chance that you could live well into your fifties or beyond. It is believed that ancient Greek philosophers and politicians lived an average of fifty-six years with some perhaps living as long as eighty. One study showed that Italian Renaissance painters lived an average of sixty-three years.[3] But being wealthy was basically a requirement for long life. Ninety-five percent of people in pre-industrial times lived in poverty and therefore didn't have access to a consistent source of food and were forced to perform types of work that quickly wore out a body. These conditions don't lead to long lifespans. Only a small portion of the populace was able to grow old.

Those of our ancestors who did grow old didn't stop working altogether but shifted to types of work that required less physical strength and stress. For instance, women who could no longer work in the fields of a farm took on more domestic duties such as overseeing young children. A study of the New England colonial era found that aging property owners continued to stay actively involved in the farm or other work done on their property by supervising family members or others who provided labor.[4] We still see this dynamic in many developing societies around the world. People continue to contribute to the community until the very end of life when their bodies stop functioning altogether.

It wasn't until the late nineteenth century and the advent of the Industrial Revolution that average lifespans started increasing. Thanks to better access to food, improving healthcare, and relatively easier work (for some), more people were able to live longer. This challenged families and communities, who began to have difficulty caring for the growing number of older people.

Work Changes

More impactfully, the nature and location of work also changed during this period. Instead of living in small communities and farms where people were able to transition to less physical work as the younger generation became able to take over, people lived in cities without small community support structures and worked in factories that required specific types of manually intensive labor. Once they were unable to work on the factory line, there weren't many other types of work that they could do.

This coincided with some of the early scientific studies on aging. Around the start of the twentieth century, studies began to emerge documenting the loss of productivity that occurred as people aged. An influential study done in 1905 by a professor of medicine at Johns Hopkins argued that by age sixty men should retire because they had lost all "mental elasticity." A subsequent English study stated that older workers lacked the adaptability needed to work in an era of rapid technological change.[5]

In response, governmental and business institutions around the world began to settle on the age of sixty-five as the age at which people should stop working. Germany adopted sixty-five as the retirement age in 1883 and others soon followed. In 1890, the U.S. set sixty-five as the age at which Union Army veterans could begin receiving pensions. In 1920, postal workers became eligible for retirement benefits. And of course, in 1934, the Commission on Economic Security created the Social Security system so that all Americans could theoretically stop working at sixty-five.

The result of this was a mass exodus from the workforce by older Americans. From 1850 (and presumably before) through 1880, nearly 80 percent of men over the age of sixty-five were gainfully employed. From 1880 through 1930, as various pension plans were created, the percentage of men sixty-five and over participating in the workforce gradually declined to 60 percent. After the creation of Social Security, the decline accelerated, reaching only 25 percent by the end of the twentieth century.

For the first time in history, our society decided that there should be a time in life when we stop working. Further, we put in systems to not only support but sometimes force people to retire from work. The problem is that while we have provided the financial support for many people to stop working, we completely ignored people's psychological need to create value and contribute. For all of human history, people transitioned the type of work they did to contribute to their family and community but never stopped contributing altogether. Now we were being told that after a certain age we were no longer able to contribute.

The result has been considerable psychological issues for those who stop working. Retirees are more likely to experience depression compared to those who are still working—28 percent of retirees report being depressed,[6] substantially higher than the 8.3 percent reported for the overall older adult population.[7] Former retiree and current entrepreneur George Jerjian conducted a survey of more than fifteen thousand retirees, asking them about the biggest challenge they faced in retirement.[8] The most common answers included:

"I miss doing the work that I love."

"I want to go back to (my profession)."

"I'm not sure what to do with my time."

"I feel lost."

"(Not) adding value to the world."

"Fear of losing my identity created over a lifetime."

"People do not see you anymore."

It turns out that for many if not most people, much of the meaning they find in life is from their profession. When they stop working, they have difficulty finding a new source of meaning.[9]

Countless resources have been created to help people navigate the psychologically difficult transition from working to retirement. Not surprisingly, the answer is often found in helping retirees find new ways to contribute to those around them. Sometimes this involves re-entering the workforce on a full- or part-time basis.[10] Often though, solving the psychological need to contribute doesn't require being paid for it. The satisfaction of contributing to the welfare of another person is what really does it.

A Center for National and Community Service (CNCS) study found that 70 percent of retirees who were prone to depression experienced fewer symptoms one year after beginning to volunteer. People over fifty who volunteer a hundred hours a year or more had a 44 percent lower risk of dying and a 17 percent lower risk of limitations in physical functioning than those who did not volunteer.[11]

It's not only older people who have stopped working. The overall labor participation rate has plummeted over the past fifty years.

The great wealth of our country has enabled a substantial number of people to simply opt out of the traditional economy. Many of these are undoubtedly doing work that is difficult for economists to measure (the advance of the gig economy has accelerated this), but there are also people whose livelihoods are supported by the largesse of loved ones or social safety nets.

Not surprisingly, depression among those out of the workforce is much higher than among those who are working. A big part of this is people who want to work but can't. They are not only faced with the challenges of surviving and providing for their families, but they are also dealing with the shame of being unemployed. Social safety nets like welfare and food stamps may help with some of the physical problems, but left unresolved are the psychological problems associated with not working and creating value.

But it's not just in people who are struggling to get by where you see this play out. The problems associated with having no outlet for creating value can be seen on the other end of the financial spectrum in so-called trust fund babies. People are fascinated with watching the train-wreck lives of those who were given so much money that they never have to work. Searching for some form of fulfillment, they spend their time on activities that only consume the work created by others. They have no outlet that satisfies their need to contribute and so live in a futile attempt to fill that void through consumption.

Life is hard. And it has always been hard. For most of history, it was much harder to merely survive, but there are still many hard parts of life today. We face incredible issues of not only providing for our family, but of also ensuring the survival of our communities in a world that is rapidly changing around us. We have been hardwired with the desire to solve problems that will make things better for ourselves and those around us. When we deny or ignore this, we suffer.

Changing the Scoreboard

It is clearly worthwhile to pursue a career that directly allows us to live our life's purpose. We spend a significant amount of our time in our jobs, and it seems a great waste to spend such a significant portion of our lives doing activities that don't contribute to or are even contrary to our purpose. If this is where you are, my guess is that by this point in the book you have already begun thinking about how to make a change.

It may be that you don't need to change jobs, but merely change the way you approach your job. As we discussed earlier, seeing your activities through the lens of your purpose often yields an understanding of how to live your purpose in your activities. Thinking about how you can live your purpose in your job will almost certainly change not only the way you think and feel about your job, but also likely the way you perform it. You may find meaning in your job that you didn't know was there before, which could improve your feeling of satisfaction in your career.

But as we think about living a purposeful life, it is also of vital importance that we understand the purpose of work itself. Yes, we must work to provide the necessities of life, but once we get past the point of earning enough to provide for the physical needs of ourselves and our loved ones, the reasons we continue to work change.

There has been so much written decrying so-called workaholism— people whose time and energy are completely consumed by their jobs. They ignore and deny other people and parts of their life and solely focus on the activities that earn them money.

Rightly so, much of the criticism of workaholics is that they are chasing satisfaction in fleeting things like wealth. Stories of Ebenezer Scrooge counting his coins alone on Christmas Eve warn us against the fallacy of seeking meaning in money.

But while I hear many people warn against over-working, I don't hear many talk about why so many people find meaning in their work to begin with. Certainly, many people focus on their job as part of a misaligned way of defining their worth. But for many people—and especially those who are highly successful in their jobs—working is about more than the money.

Recently I had a conversation with a friend in the commercial insurance industry. He is tremendously successful and absolutely loves what he does. I listened to him one night describe the thrill he still gets in closing a deal.

"What we do is so complex, and I must lead a team of people who are experts in so many different areas to come up with something that solves a big enough problem for my customer that they will spend huge sums of money to solve it," he said. "The money is nice, but I still love the feeling of putting all that together."

I have heard similar comments from so many successful businesspeople. At some point, it stops being about the money and is just about the work itself—they love getting to compete and solve big problems. They are addicted to the feeling of overcoming challenges and seeing the results of their efforts.

As we counsel people to be wary of the perils of putting too much of their time and energy into their work, we should not discourage the instinct that is driving that behavior—the need to create value. While that need is certainly much bigger for some people than others, it is a need that every human has at some level. Instead of making people feel guilty about the misguided satisfaction they find through their work—"oh, you just love money/fame/attention/power!"—why not instead invite people to focus their drive to create value in ways that are directed at fulfilling their purpose?

Like it or not, the primary way our society recognizes someone's worth is through professional achievements. Despite all the cheesy gifts given on Father's Day, no one actually gives out an award for "Dad of the Year," but there are lots of awards for Salesperson, Executive, Entrepreneur, Entertainer, or Player of the Year. People don't get rich by being amazing at meditation; they earn money by providing something of value through work.

For us to live purposefully in every part of our life, we must see the way we measure our success through a lens that may be different from what others around us use. We must leverage our desire and ability to create value toward achieving something different than the typical societal measures of success.

One nice thing about sports is that it is easy to determine who wins. If you are playing baseball, whoever has more runs at the end of the game wins. When we begin to look at the way we work through the lens of our purpose, our definition of winning may differ from that of others. In other words, we need to change the scoreboard.

Bob Buford was a very successful CEO of a family-owned company that owned a network of cable systems across the country and decided to pivot his focus to challenging and inspiring leaders to think differently about why they work. In 1995, Buford wrote a book called *Halftime: Moving from Success to Significance*. In the book, Buford challenges people who are looking at the second half of life not to stop working, but to think differently about the outcome of their work:

> After a first half of building a career and trying to become financially secure, we'd like to do something in the second half that is more meaningful. . . . As we move closer to the halftime of our lives, we realize that we can only buy, sell, manage, and attain so much. We also begin to understand that we will live only so long. When all is said and done, our success will be pretty empty unless it has included a corresponding degree of significance.[12]

What does it mean to do something significant? What should be your scoreboard for success? What does it look like for you to fulfill your purpose through your work? Those are questions only you can answer.

Summing It Up

So what do we do with all of this? I get that I'm wired to work, but how do I think about work's role in my life?

Here are three things to consider:

1. Be conscious of *how* you are fulfilling your need to work. See your work activities through the lens of your purpose. Hopefully, you can have a vocation that clearly allows you to do purposeful things, but if not, make sure you are making time for activities that fulfill your need to create and contribute.

2. Remember that the satisfaction of work comes from doing things that contribute to our welfare and the welfare of the people around us on whom we depend and who depend on us. Don't fall into the trap of assuming that the only way of satisfying your need to work is through a job. The ways of creating value are as numerous as there are people to do them. The feeling of accomplishment one gets from value creation can come from creating music, making a meal, being a mentor, or lending a listening ear.

3. And if you are highly gifted at creating value that leads to the accumulation of wealth, think about what your work is contributing to. If it doesn't match your values, consider switching things up and taking on work that is consistent with your purpose. Then, consider using that same drive to achieve not only at work, but also in every other part of your life.

CHAPTER 16

About Relationships

IN 1938, HARVARD BEGAN tracking the health of 268 students. The scope of the project was ambitious and one that only an institution with the long-term stability of Harvard could attempt, as the researchers intended to follow these young men throughout their lives. Their goal was to discover clues as to what caused people to live happy and healthy lives. The researchers later added to the cohort by taking over a research project that was begun around the same time that followed boys who had grown up in a tenement area of Boston. Though interest and funding has waxed and waned through the decades, the study has continued largely unabated to present day and has expanded to include the wives and children of the original men, with plans to move on to their grandchildren and great-grandchildren.

When the study was launched, the expectation for the results seems to have been influenced by the beliefs of the time in biological determinism—that genetics determines success in life (this belief was influential in the formation of eugenics). The study's founder was a physician named Arlie Bock who ran health services at Harvard University. Bock believed that medical research focused too much on sick people and as such would never be able to answer the question of how to live well. His study would focus on students who could "paddle their own canoe" and "attempt to analyze the forces that have produced normal young men," thus setting the criteria for the original 268 subjects.[1]

The study started well before the advent of DNA testing (which current participants undergo), so researchers performed analysis on the subjects typical of the times and reflective of their deterministic view—including among other things anthropometric measuring of skulls and facial features, examining organ function, and tracking brain activity. They hypothesized that a combination of intellectual ability, physical makeup, and personality traits would be revealed as the secret formula.[2]

The history of the Harvard study reads like a textbook detailing the progression of psychological theories during the twentieth century. As new directors and researchers took over the project, their views on psychological health revealed themselves in the questions they asked participants in the ongoing surveys whose frequency reflected the funding status of the project at the time. One particularly interesting survey in the 1960s included a focus on smoking, with a question about brand preference of cigarettes—most likely inserted for the benefit of the project's sponsor during that time, Phillip Morris.

Reading the reports generated throughout the study reveals clues as to the ultimate lessons learned, but it really took being able to track the entire lifespan of these individuals before researchers could see the whole story. Some participants who started at the bottom of the socioeconomic ladder climbed all the way up, while others who started at the top fell all the way down. Participants got divorced, succumbed to psychological disease like schizophrenia, committed suicide, and many died from issues around alcoholism. Several lived to old age, continually living what appeared to researchers as happy, contented lives, regularly scoring high on health and wellness indices.

So after analyzing thousands of subjects from varying backgrounds with varying levels of intelligence, education, and wealth, what did the data show?

George Vaillant was the study's third and longest-serving director. In his book *Aging Well*, Vaillant says that the Harvard study revealed several factors that lend toward living a healthier and happier life, including physical activity, absence of alcohol abuse and smoking, mature mechanisms to cope with life's ups and downs, and a healthy body weight. Education is an additional factor, but mostly because education tends to lead people toward exhibiting more of those healthy behaviors.[3]

However, there was one factor that not only surpassed those others but also could cause them.

"When the study began, nobody cared about empathy or attachment," Vaillant said. "But the key to healthy aging is relationships, relationships, relationships."

The study's fourth (and current) director, psychiatrist Dr. Robert Waldinger, put it this way: "The surprising finding is that our relationships and how happy we are in our relationships has a powerful influence on our health. Taking care of your body is important, but tending to your relationships is a form of self-care too. That, I think, is the revelation."[4]

Amazingly, having deeply satisfying relationships not only impacts our mental health but also our physical health. Waldinger goes on to say: "When we gathered together everything we knew about them at age fifty, it wasn't their middle-age cholesterol levels that predicted how they were going to grow old. It was how satisfied they were in their relationships. The people who were the most satisfied in their relationships at age fifty were the healthiest at age eighty."[5]

The opposite is also true. The absence of warm relationships causes health problems. "Loneliness kills," Waldinger adds. "It's as powerful as smoking or alcoholism."[6]

Waldinger's observation from the Harvard study about loneliness has been found by other studies as well. The National Academies of Sciences, Engineering, and Medicine conducted a large study on the impacts of social isolation and loneliness. They found that social isolation, which they define as "an objective lack of social contact with others," significantly increased a person's risk of premature death from all causes and lead to a 50 percent increased risk of dementia.[7] Loneliness, defined as "the subjective feeling of being isolated," was associated with higher rates of depression, anxiety, and suicide, a 29 percent increase in the risk of heart disease, and a 32 percent increased risk of stroke. Like Waldinger, the NASEM's authors liken the results of loneliness and its impact on your body to those of smoking, obesity, and physical inactivity.[8]

Consider that for a moment. It is arguably better for your health to be a chain smoker than to spend your life without meaningful relationships. How can this be?

Needing Others

The creation story in the Bible concludes as God has just created man. The man was living in a paradise where he was safe and food was readily available. He had seen and named every animal. And yet God said, "It is not good that the man should be alone."[9] So God caused the man to fall into a deep sleep and created a woman.

Humans are innately social creatures. From the beginning of time, we have formed groups necessary to survive. Being alone meant being unprotected. It meant that there was no one to guard you when you were asleep. That there would be no one to take care of you if you got hurt.

Further, we quickly realized that we had to cooperate with others to get things we needed for ourselves. One person couldn't defeat a woolly mammoth, but a group of several people could take one down and eat for days.

One of the most severe punishments for bad behavior in ancient times was to be cast out of the community and into the wilderness. Doing so was akin to a death sentence because everyone realized how difficult it was to survive alone. We mimic this today when we put our most violent criminals in solitary confinement. One could argue that being forced to be alone, not death, is the ultimate punishment.

When people live in very small groups where everyone is well-known, it is obvious who is trustworthy and carrying their own weight. Accountability is quick when someone doesn't do their part to support the group, so there tends to be higher levels of social pressure to be reliable in playing one's part in making sure the group survives.

As our ancestors began to gather in bigger and bigger groups (villages, towns, and cities), they encountered situations where they didn't know everyone. Suddenly their well-being could be impacted by someone they didn't know. They had to develop more sophisticated skills to determine who could be counted on. In other words, we had to learn how to determine who our friends were. Further, we had to learn behaviors that would ensure others would want to stay our friends.

The physical reality that we needed others to survive caused us to develop deep psychological desires to be in community with others.

While most of us don't need other people to help protect us from a wild animal trying to hunt us down, we still need other people for physical survival. No one can produce all the things necessary for survival over an extended period. And even if they could, if they ever got hurt or sick and were therefore unable to work, they would have no one to care for them and would quickly perish. The reality is that we need each other just as much today as our ancestors who roamed the savannah. Even if we aren't consciously aware of this, the response we see from our mind and our body when our relationships are healthy or unhealthy tells us so.

Family

The desire to procreate is one of the most powerful psychological forces that impacts people. At a practical level, people historically needed children as an extra set of hands to help them survive. The aid that could be provided by children after they grew was so great that it was worth the years of extra effort spent in caring for these largely helpless beings. They also knew that the children were the most likely to be counted on to care for them in old age when they were no longer able to care for themselves.

But even for our ancestors, the desire for progeny went way beyond building a retirement plan. Our deep psychological desire to matter and to leave a mark on the world beyond our lifetime reveals itself when we behold our child. Most parents will tell you that the immensity of the emotions they have for their children is beyond almost anything else they have experienced. It is no wonder that the relationships between the two people who produce children and with the children themselves are the strongest relational bonds that most people ever have.

Children are psychologically important for parents, but parents are vital for children. Way beyond just providing for physical survival while they are young and vulnerable, parents teach children how to survive on their own—physically and psychologically. When parents do this ineffectively it is disastrous for the child. When they aren't there at all, it is devastating.

Foster children live in difficult circumstances that are not of their own making. When a child is put into foster care, it is because they don't have a parent who is capable of caring for them. This generally means that they have experienced abuse, neglect, or both.

Many amazing people devote themselves to caring for these endangered children. They serve as foster parents, mentors, and caregivers who try to step into the void these kids are experiencing by not having parents in their life. There are many wonderful stories of children who are adopted into other families as well as many who are successfully reunited with birth parents who have been able to work through troubles of their own. While many of them carry great burdens into adulthood from the trauma they have endured, many of these kids are able to build resilience and live happy, healthy lives.

But a lot of foster kids don't get new families or become reunited with their original ones. Many bounce from home to home, never connecting with anyone who can care for them. Then, at the age of eighteen, the government declares them an adult and they "age out"—meaning they no longer have access to the resources provided by the foster care system. They suddenly find themselves solely responsible for their own care. They must provide for their own food and shelter without the support of anyone else. Not surprisingly, most of them fail.

What happens to the twenty-three thousand children who age out of the foster care system every year? The National Foster Youth Institute tracks the following datapoints:

- 20 percent will be instantly homeless.
- Only half will find gainful employment by the age of 24.
- 7 out of 10 girls will become pregnant before the age of 21.
- 60 percent of young men will be convicted of a crime.
- Half will develop a substance abuse problem.

- 1 in 4 will not graduate high school or obtain a GED.

- 25 percent will suffer from the direct effects of post-traumatic stress disorder.

- Just 3 percent will earn a college degree at some point in their lives.

- 75 percent of women and 33 percent of men will receive government benefits to meet basic needs.[10]

Think about those statistics. More than half of young men who had no consistent parental figures in their life will spend time in jail. That is an astounding number.

Government programs can provide physical protection, food, and shelter for a time, but these kids aren't struggling later in life because they missed meals; they are struggling because no one taught them how to live. They need direction, discipline, teaching, guidance, advice, and ultimately the friendship that only genuinely devoted adults can give.

Children need parents.

But adults have so much to gain from their families as well. More than just the continuance of their last name or someone to give them a ride to the retirement home, family can provide incredible comfort and meaningful relationships.

During the writing of this book, my wife and I have been transitioning from having kids who live at home to kids who are leaving the nest. It can be an emotional, heart-rending process to see someone you have nurtured for eighteen years go out on their own. Luckily, we have had wise mentors who are just ahead of us in this process.

"Trust us," they told us, "As wonderful as it was when they were young, it can be even better when they are older. Our kids have become the most amazing people and we just love being with them, being friends with them."

We trade the joy of the four-year-old running to us when we get home for the adult who is driving to us because he wants to spend time together. It's not a bad trade.

Regardless of whether you are a parent, there is nothing quite like the warm feeling of being surrounded by those who love us. They are the people we know that, even if we haven't seen them in months or years, would drop everything to come and help us if we were in need. They are the ones who cheer for us no matter what, see potential in us that even we don't see, and won't hesitate to jump to our defense. There is generally no security like that which can be found in familial relationships.

Which is why there is nothing quite as painful as being shunned by family. When the people who are supposed to have my back don't show up or give up on me, it can shake me to the core. If I can't rely on my family, who can I rely on? If even my family doesn't care about me, what does that mean about me?

Realizing that my family has the ability to cause such a great span of emotions in me, means that I can do the same for them. Investing in relationships with my family is among the very best things I can do for them—and for me.

Friends

My kids were young when we were in the throes of building our business. During this time, all of my focus was on work and my immediate family. I was determined to help make the company successful and was unwilling to sacrifice being a great dad. Choosing to focus on those things meant I had to say no to a lot of other things—including personal friends. Old friendships drifted away as I put little time into them, and I found myself left with only family and professional relationships.

While this period of life was highly rewarding in many ways, the lack of personal friendships began to take a toll. My wife encouraged me to seek friends (even setting us up on "double dates" with other couples). However, our business began to get some notoriety and, as the public face of the company, people often see me as a way to get a job, sell something, or just take advantage of me to get something they wanted. I went through a difficult period where I became highly skeptical of anyone I met, and specifically of anyone who wanted to meet me. That skepticism began to turn to cynicism (is there no one who doesn't want something from me?) and self-doubt (what's wrong with me that I can't make friends?).

Someone I knew suggested to me that I consider joining a group that assembles people who are in a similar phase of life. I resisted for a while, but eventually my wife convinced me to join. She could see how not having friends was impacting me and us.

That decision changed my life. For more than a decade since, I have spent a day a month with a group of men who have nothing to gain from me other than my friendship. They have no ulterior motives—nothing to sell to me and they don't need a job. Since they are going through similar challenges as me, we can identify and empathize with each other in a way that few people can. We have ultimate confidence that we will be respected and accepted and so are able to share our intimate fears, hopes, and dreams.

All of us need friends. Throughout our history, people have had to figure out who we can trust for mutual protection—our friends. When we don't have friends, when we are alone, our body intuitively knows there is a problem. The primordial areas of our brain know that being alone is dangerous, and so our anxiety goes up as we search for danger. We don't sleep well, our blood pressure goes up, and we become more aggressive, depressed, and withdrawn. When our anxiety stays high for extended periods of time, those symptoms cause long-term health problems that lead to higher mortality.[11]

Incredibly, just being around friends can have an immediate physical impact—our blood pressure goes down and we are better at handling stress.[12] The hug or touch of a friend triggers hormones in the reward centers of the brain that make us want to make these relationships stronger. Once again, the body rewards what it knows we need to survive.

In Lydia Denworth's seminal work *Friendship*, she explains a study done at the University of Chicago on the physiological impact of friends:

> Just as hunger signals us that we need to eat, perhaps loneliness (is) a warning bell designed to make us want to be with others, the social equivalent of physical pain, hunger, and thirst. Evolution fashioned us not only to feel good when connected but to feel secure. The vitally important corollary is that evolution shaped us not only to feel bad in isolation but to feel insecure, as in physically threatened. . . . Isolation makes us feel unsafe.[13]

Denworth explains that a quality relationship must have three things: It's a stable, longstanding bond; it's positive; and it's cooperative. Friendships are helpful and reciprocal. "I'm there for you; you're there for me."[14]

Over the past few years, physicians and health experts have become more focused on the "social determinants of health." These are the environmental factors that affect a person's health, functioning, and quality of life. Social determinants include things like economic stability, access to healthcare, access to education, and living in a safe environment.

Friends impact virtually all of these. Friends help you when you lose your job. They give you a ride to the hospital when you are sick. They pick up your kids from school so you can work, and your child can get an education. And they help you keep the neighborhood safe.

A few years ago, my mother and stepfather volunteered to watch our young kids so my wife and I could go on a rare vacation together. While we were gone, my mother fell and had to go to the hospital for what ended up being several days. Our young children were stuck in the hospital waiting room with no one to care for them as we were thousands of miles and at least two days of travel away.

My wife called her best friend and could barely finish explaining what happened before she and her husband were in the car to go get our kids. They took them into their home, fed them, got them to school, and kept them safe.

About a year later, those same friends were out of town when their house caught on fire. Since we live only about a mile away from each other, my wife was the first one on the scene. Unfortunately, there was nothing that could be done, and they lost everything they owned. This time it was our turn to take them into our home, providing some of the basic items they had lost just so they could survive the first few days.

We don't make friends just as an insurance policy for potential emergency scenarios, but those scenarios are inevitable, and when they happen, our friends are who we turn to. That's why our bodies and brains go on alert when we feel alone.

It turns out that it's not just close friends that are important to us. Casual friends, even acquaintances, can be vitally important in many circumstances. The more people we can access in our wider network the more likely we are to find someone who has already experienced and learned how to handle a particular problem we are facing. Our expanded networks give us access to resources, introductions, information, and ideas that we would miss out on if we were limited to only our close friends. In fact, studies have shown that the more people you have in your network, the happier you are likely to be—especially if those people are happy.[15]

The Ebb and Flow of Relationships

There is no formula for the number and type of friends you should have. Friendships reflect our individuality—some people have just a few close friends and others have many friends. Some people naturally build bigger networks and others don't. Friendships ebb and flow, come and go during seasons of life. The friends of our youth are rarely the friends of adulthood. Those we were close to when we were single may drift away when we have a family. Our close friends from our old neighborhood may become less intimate after we move. Some friends move out of our life, only to come back later.

Of course, friendships can also be bad for us. We have all had the friend who we would say was a negative influence. Friends can get us up to go to the gym at 5:30 in the morning, but they can also convince us to stay at the bar too late and drink more than we should.

When viewed through the lens of purpose, friends and family aren't just people to have fun with and that we hope will be there for us when there is an emergency. Friends can help us in our purpose journey or set us back. We should ask how we can live our purpose in each relationship, and how each relationship helps us live our purpose. The answer to those questions may radically alter how and even whether we invest time and energy into certain people.

Living our purpose could mean investing more time with someone who helps us live purposely. It may mean ending a relationship that distracts us from our purpose. It might mean spending significant amounts of time with someone who can give us nothing in return. Caring for a sick family member or aging parent is one of the most selfless investments we can make, yet that person can give none of the quid pro quo typical of most relationships. We may get nothing but the satisfaction of having selflessly cared for someone else. When we are in those seasons, we desperately need other close friends who can care for us.

Friendships are vital, but they don't just happen. Friendships must be earned. While we have many words that are assigned to designate the category of a relationship (colleague, brother, cousin, boss), the word friend is bestowed. Describing someone as a friend is to point out the quality, character, and history of the relationship. It is an emotionally laden term. Introducing someone as "my colleague" is very different than saying "my colleague and my friend."

Spouses

Sitting at the intersection of friends and family is perhaps the most important relationship for many—our spouses. This most intimate of relationships goes beyond friendship to companionship. A companion is a person with whom you spend a lot of time because you are traveling together. A spouse—our chosen companion—is the person with whom we travel the journey of life.

Over the past few decades, the institution of marriage has sometimes been labeled as antiquated and not necessary, but it turns out that marriage is the strongest determining factor of happiness for Americans. Researchers in 2022 validated once again something that has been known for centuries—that being married makes you much more likely to be happy—30 percent more likely. In fact, the only people more likely to be happy than married people are married people with children.[16]

This is surprising but shouldn't be. When we have a companion whom we can trust to help us and care for us, it satisfies our deepest need for safety and security. Of all our relationships, our life companion is the one most worthy of investing in because it has the best possible return.

One of the most powerful and important questions we need to answer for our own psychological well-being is, "Who will help me when I am helpless?" The need to answer that question is fundamental to our basic feelings of security. As selfish as it may seem, devoting time and energy to building our closest relationships builds tremendous security and is one of the best things you can do for yourself.

But creating reciprocal, long-standing, positive relationships requires intentional focus and an investment of time and energy. We must choose to invest in relationships. I'll let Denworth have the last word:

> Hard as it is for individuals to change our habits, we are not absolved of responsibility. We must make friendship a priority and factor it into the way we plan our time—and our children's time. Yes, you can choose your friends, but you must also more generally choose friendship—embrace it, invest in it, work at it. Put time and attention into building quality relationships. You cannot afford not to.[17]

CHAPTER 17

About Self

YOU ARE THE ONLY person you will have to spend the rest of your life with. Your colleagues, your neighbors, your family, your spouse— they will be in your life for a while, but chances are that many or most of them won't be there until the end. And even those people are only with you some of the time. You are stuck with yourself all the time.

Apparently, for many of us, "stuck" is the right term as we don't seem to like the person who greets us in the mirror every morning. Americans spend nearly $70 billion a year on cosmetic surgery to alter their appearance. We spend another $150 billion on products designed to help us lose weight. This doesn't even include gym memberships, but only products such as soft gels, tablets, capsules, powders, gummies, jellies, premixes, liquids, and others. We spend $15 billion on candy, $10 billion on ice cream, and $11 billion on potato chips. Could we save a lot of money if we stopped buying the $36 billion worth of junk food and thus negate the need for the $150 billion on the drugs to counteract it?

We spend a lot of money to improve not only what we see on the outside but also what we feel on the inside. The "self-improvement" industry of books, coaches, and apps is estimated at $13 billion. Motivational speakers rake in about $1.8 billion a year.[1]

Perhaps much of the money we spend trying to change or better ourselves is because we don't have a proper view of ourselves.

In the *Iliad*, Homer tells the tragic tale of Niobe, a princess who was married to Amphion, the king of Thebes. The royal couple had fourteen children—seven sons and seven daughters—a sign of great blessing for a queen.

At a ceremony held to honor the goddess Leto, the mother of Apollo and Artemis, Niobe began to brag about how she was superior to Leto, who had only two children compared to her fourteen. Apollo and Artemis were enraged to hear this bragging and came down to earth to kill Niobe's children—Apollo killing the boys and Artemis killing the girls.

Devastated, King Amphion killed himself, leaving Niobe completely alone and in deep anguish having lost her entire family. Hearing her pleading for the gods to end her pain, Zeus had compassion and turned her into a rock—to turn her feelings to stone.

However, even as a rock she continued to cry, with her tears coming out of the stone. Today, people can see her image and tears as they seep out of the porous limestone rock on a cliff of Mount Sipylus in Turkey.

Investing in Yourself

Ancient mythologies and religions are full of stories warning us against hubris—excessive pride or self-confidence. Our English word *hubris* comes from the Greek word *hybris*, which involves putting oneself at odds with the nature of things by assuming a role or status that is reserved for the gods. The punishment by the gods on humans who had exhibited hybris was to remind them of their human limitations and mortality.

We started this book with a stark look at our own mortality and how our actions and existence will be forgotten in time. We have considered how insignificant we are as only a speck in the universe and one of billions in our own world. We studied how the only way to matter, to be able to show we made any difference from our life, is through our impact and service to others.

Yet, we also have talked about our future self as someone worth considering. We have spent much time in reflection on who we are—delving into our strengths, passions, and what gives us joy. We have considered how we can find meaning through the ripples that we leave.

So what gives? Which is it? Should we focus on ourselves or not? Should we do things that make us feel good or things that are good for others? Should we think highly of ourselves or see ourselves as insignificant?

The answer is yes.

It is tempting to think that the antidote to hubris is complete self-denial, but thinking too little of yourself can be just as damaging as thinking too much. If you don't believe this, just ask your friends.

When I am weak or unhealthy, other people pay the price. Being sick results in my being unable to do things for myself, and others must pick up the slack. When I am weak, someone else has to deal with the ramifications of my weakness. If I'm sick, my wife has to take on my chores and do double duty. If she's too weak to lift something, it means that I have to lift it.

Likewise, when you are psychologically or emotionally weak or unhealthy, other people in your life suffer. When I am quick-tempered, my colleagues will feel the wrath. If I lack self-confidence, my friends must provide constant reassurance. If I am constantly dealing with anxiety, my family will hide problems so as to not push me over the edge.

Any marriage counselor will tell you that a healthy marriage requires two healthy people. You cannot fulfill your role of loving and serving a spouse if you are consumed by damaging habits caused by unresolved issues. For me to lay down my life to serve you means I must have a life to lay down.

One of the best things you can do for your family and friends (and for parents your children) is to be the best you. Investing in yourself isn't only a gift to your present and future you, it is a gift to all those in the present and future who need you. Perhaps more than a gift, it is a moral obligation. Just like you want and need others who are capable of watching your back, others need you to be strong and healthy enough to watch their back. Healthy relationships are reciprocal relationships, so you must be healthy enough to reciprocate.

Physical Self

I haven't seen your personal purpose statement, but I doubt that the way you described how you will live the most joyful version of your life includes descriptors like: lethargic, unable to physically do things I enjoy, dependent on medication to function, forgetful, and embarrassed of how I look.

Like it or not, we are not only spiritual beings but also physical. The condition of our body directly impacts our quality of life and our ability to protect and serve those we care about. Yet, the way that many people treat their bodies demonstrates that they are content to be sick and helpless now or in the future.

The scientific evidence for physical activity couldn't be more clear. According to the National Institutes of Health, physical activity leads to physical benefits like improved functional capacity and decreased risks of diseases, but it also leads to increased life satisfaction and happiness.[2]

The reasoning behind this is obvious—your body was designed to move and do work. The phenomenon of sitting around in a chair all day was completely unknown to our ancestors. If they weren't doing some sort of physical labor it meant that they were going to starve. Again, the body recognizes and rewards what it needs.

Have you ever heard someone describe the "runner's high"? Or talk about that almost euphoric feeling after completing a workout? That's their body saying "Good job! You did some work so that means we'll be able to eat tomorrow!" Physical activity isn't just to keep your body healthy; your mind needs it too.

Any definition of purposeful living must include a purposeful plan to care for your body. Ignoring your physical health is one of the most destructive things you can do to yourself and those you love.

Defining Physical Health

There are many great resources to help us understand how to improve our physical health. There is also a lot of misinformation and plain junk. I will not attempt to answer every question about physical health here (nor am I qualified to do so anyway), but I will give some principles that I have found helpful in discerning which practices are true and helpful.

- Like anything, it is important to define success. My goal for my physical health is to live in such a way that I can thrive physically now and in the future. This means that I am strong enough, flexible enough, mobile enough, and healthy enough to do the physical things I enjoy. It also means that I am incorporating practices that will pre-pare my body to be as healthy as it can be during the last decade of my life. This means that I won't consider any

diets, workouts, chemicals, or surgical procedures that
may yield short-term gains but cause long-term damage.

- Focus on diet and not "Diets." Learn about the chemistry
of the food you are eating and the impact it has not just
on your waistline but on your brain. The more likely it is
to have come from a farm or ocean and not from a factory, the better it is bound to be. If you can't pronounce
the ingredients, it's unlikely your ancestors passed on to
you the genes necessary to effectively utilize it as energy.
Diets that propose quick dramatic results by eliminat-
ing vital nutritional elements aren't sustainable and most
likely do long-term damage. At the end of the day, you
can't go wrong by cutting sugar (in all forms), consuming
fewer calories, and eating more vegetables.

- Your ancestors moved all the time. Your body was made
to work, and it assumes you are going to do physical
activity that burns the calories it takes in. If you are
sedentary, then your body starts working against you. As
Dr. Peter Attia says, "Exercise is by far the most potent
longevity 'drug.' No other intervention does nearly as
much to prolong our lifespan and preserve our cogni-
tive and physical function."[3] And by the way, if you call
it "exercise," it is probably something you don't enjoy,
will have a hard time sustaining, or isn't good for you
anyway. Seek out physical activities that are rewarding
enough to keep you coming back.

- Sleep. No really. Sleep. Live in such a way that you are
tired at night and wake up naturally when you are rested
and ready to face the day. Whatever amount of sleep you
get now is probably not as much as your body needs. You
cannot overestimate the impact getting enough sleep can
have on your health.

- Drinking lots of alcohol regularly is really bad for you. Not just because of your headache the next morning. Alcohol has a compounding effect that impacts your physical and mental capacity over time. Recent studies are showing that any alcohol use has negative long-term effects, but I'm pretty sure that drinking a bourbon while sitting around a campfire with your friends is so good for you that it counteracts whatever it is those studies show.

Emotional Self

Never in my life before or since have I felt such confusion and bewilderment than at that moment. I knew nothing about what was happening. I had no context to identify with the situation and no idea how to respond. I was, in a word, afraid.

So when the hormone-raged crying, screaming, laughing, and crying again emotional outburst was over, I looked away from my early-adolescent daughter toward my wife and said, "I don't understand any of this."

Now, I'm not advocating that any of us go on crying, screaming rants, but there may actually be something to be learned from early-adolescent girls—they feel all the feelings. As adults, we like to ignore our feelings or at least pretend they don't matter.

I once read an author who argued that all decisions are emotionally driven. There are no rational decision-makers. Rational decisions are just emotional decisions disguised with carefully selected facts and arguments that justify the decision we already made based on our emotions.

Now, I'm not sure I completely agree with that assessment, but it certainly points to the incredible weight that our emotions have on our actions. In chapter 9, we talked about reacting versus responding, and how the pause we take to respond allows us to consider the emotions that are driving how we would have reacted.

This practice of considering your emotions is incredibly difficult. First, I need the time to consider how I really feel about a situation. Then I get to the daunting task of answering, "Why do I feel the way I do?"

I like to think of myself as a mature person who has a great perspective on life and on what's important. I am generally calm and considered in my actions. Except when I am watching a sporting event. Especially if one of my kids is playing. Then I become a complete idiot. One time on the ride home from a game, my wife said to me, "You know how you make fun of those loud, obnoxious dads who scream and complain the whole game? That was pretty much you tonight."

I gotta tell you that hurt. What was worse is that as I thought about it, she was right.

And there's nothing worse than when your wife is right.

I spent the rest of the night thinking about what had happened. The things I was saying exemplified emotions like annoyance, disappointment, and maybe even anger. Why did I feel those things?

Emotions are attempts by your mind to communicate with others and ultimately cause actions that result in something you desire. But emotions always point to a motivation that caused them.

What caused those emotions at the game that day? Well, I have regret about certain things I have failed at in life and that regret has caused some shame and insecurity. Some part of my subconscious mind thought that our team winning would have made me feel stronger and less insecure because I was associated with the team.

So I was complaining about the plays our coach was calling because I feel insecure about times when I have failed.

Whoa. I should work on that.

Emotions are neither good nor bad—they just are. You can't argue with someone's emotions. Saying things like "you shouldn't feel angry" is completely ridiculous, not to mention demeaning. We may not control our emotions, but we can control how we react to our emotions and, more importantly, we can work to change the desires and insecurities that cause them in the first place.

Respecting other people's emotions means that we should also respect our own. Paying attention to your emotions includes giving yourself time to consider them—real, honest, introspective time.

It also helps to have people in our lives who love us enough to point out the impact our emotions are causing.

Passionate Self

Several of the exercises in chapter 11 were to help us identify things we are passionate about. Our passions come from a mix of our experiences, strengths, and influences, but regardless of where they come from, certain things just energize us and feel enjoyable. Some things are interesting to us and other things aren't.

When we do things we enjoy, it triggers pleasure chemicals that are good for our health. Taking part in hobbies lowers our heart rate, improves our mental outlook, and lowers our stress levels.[4] Yes, having fun is good for your health.

Somewhere along the way, many of us picked up the idea that choosing to spend time doing things we enjoy that have no benefit to anyone else was detrimentally selfish. Perhaps as an attempt to avoid becoming completely self-absorbed, we overreact by denying ourselves any activities that are "just for us." More often, situations and seasons of life have us so focused on work and relationships that there is no room for doing things we personally enjoy. We will discuss this phenomenon in the next chapter.

We cannot give our family, friends, or even our work what they need and deserve from us if we aren't healthy. If it is true that doing things we enjoy helps our mental outlook, then we have an obligation to do what we can to bring our best self to those we love by having some fun. Allowing ourselves some time for enjoyment isn't a purely selfish decision. It is recognizing that we must care for ourselves so that we can care for others.

Of course, not everything that is fun or pleasurable to us is good for us or helpful in creating the experience we want in our life. Certainly, many things that feel good in the moment have disastrous long-term consequences. Be honest with yourself and ask if you are using the need to create a positive mental outlook by doing things you enjoy as an excuse for destructive behaviors that ignore important people and responsibilities. In your heart, you know the difference between self-care and self-indulgence.

We need the self-awareness to know when our body is just so worn down that we should allow ourselves the luxury of vegging out on the couch or soaking in the tub. We also need the self-awareness to know when we are using that as an excuse to be lazy instead of doing things we enjoy that simultaneously strengthen us.

I've got an hour to myself. Do I spend it vegging out and watching a football game or reading a book? Do I read the trashy novel or the history book? I know that I need to allow time for things I enjoy, but how do I allocate that time? How do I decide what to do?

One practice I use when determining what to do with the precious time I have to myself is to ask the question, "Is this going to make me better?" Yes, just having fun makes me better, but doing something I enjoy that also broadens my understanding of the world, makes me physically stronger, or exposes me to new ideas is even more rewarding.

For at least the past fifteen years, I have chosen to attend a conference that has nothing to do directly with my job. I carve out a few days to go somewhere so that I can sit and listen to smart people talk about things I know little about. It may not sound like it to you, but I find it to be both selfish and immensely enjoyable. I am carving time away from work and family to go somewhere by myself and indulge my curiosity. I have chosen a few duds, but most of the time I come back from these trips refreshed, energized, and full of ideas. I've learned about things as varied as artificial intelligence, meditative techniques, and making bourbon. Much of what I have learned about the world and a lot of the ideas I have written about in this book have come from these excursions.

Way back in chapter 2, we talked about how we exercise choice in everything we do. There may be no more poignant opportunity for us to be purposeful in our life than what we choose to do in our personal downtime. There is no one to judge this other than you. Whatever you choose, own it.

Spiritual Self

At some point, each of us has a realization that there is something more to us than our physical bodies and sensations. That we aren't just a combination of chemical reactions that causes us to act. That our consciousness points to a spirit, a soul that is somehow intertwined with our physical self and yet separate.

We also face the reality of our world and the temporal nature of our physical self. We realize that even the best of this world is fleeting and unsatisfactory. At some deep level, that recognition creates a longing for something more. More satisfying, more lasting, more than just us. Something that is bigger than what we experience here and now. Something that connects us and yet simultaneously makes us matter. Something that points us to an existence that is better than the tarnished one we experience and create.

I will not try to convince you here of the truth of a particular religion or spiritual viewpoint. I will, however, try to convince you not to ignore that urging that causes us to ask the deep questions of our soul like "Is there something bigger than me?"

C. S. Lewis made a statement that I believe is instructive: "If the whole universe has no meaning, we should never have found out that it has no meaning: just as, if there were no light in the universe and therefore no creatures with eyes, we should never know it was dark."[5]

If there had been no light, then we would never have developed eyes and therefore would not have known there was no light because we wouldn't have eyes to allow us to understand the concept of light. Likewise, if the universe had no meaning, we wouldn't have the ability to contemplate the meaning of the universe. Said differently, the fact that we can contemplate the meaning of the universe means that it must have meaning.

As we said earlier: The fact that you exist means you have a purpose. If you didn't have a purpose, you wouldn't exist.

The point is that each of us has in us a desire to explore the deeper questions of this life and the one that is perhaps yet to come. Our spiritual self is just as or more important a part of us as our physical self. Denying ourselves time to explore spiritual matters is just as dangerous as denying ourselves food or exercise.

Solitude

German theologian Paul Tillich noted that there are two sides to being alone. "Our language . . . has created the word 'loneliness' to express the pain of being alone, and it has created the word 'solitude' to express the glory of being alone."[6]

One afternoon my wife and I were discussing something that should have been easy but wasn't. We couldn't agree and I was visibly irritated. I was being short-tempered, sarcastic, and just an overall jerk.

"When was the last time you worked out?" she asked me.

"I don't know. Probably three days ago. Why?"

"Go for a run and when you get back, we will talk about this again."

My wife knows me. She also knows how important it is for everyone, not just me, to take care of themselves—their physical, passionate, and spiritual self. And she knows that for me, running checks all those boxes. Running taxes my body, which triggers endorphins and improves my mood. I have fun as I see the beautiful parts of our neighborhood. And maybe most importantly, it gives me undistracted time by myself to just think.

When I showed back up an hour later, I was a different person— calm, relaxed, and with a proper perspective. We quickly resolved the dispute.

I don't care how extroverted or introverted you are, you need moments of solitude. You need to spend time alone so that you can drown out the other noises and have a conversation with the only person you will spend the rest of your life with: yourself. You need to pray, to meditate, or whatever gets you into a state of mind to consider what is going on in your life. You need to ask whether the things you're spending time on will benefit your future self; whether the choices you're making lead to results you consciously desire or just the ones that feel good in the moment; if your actions are serving others or only focused on yourself.

You need time with no one and nothing else to distract you— solitude—to evaluate whether you are living a life of purpose. Your purpose.

If you aren't used to it, solitude can be scary. We start panicking that we are missing something or forgetting things. We may hear this inner chatter: *Surely someone needs me or is waiting for me. My competitor is using this time to get ahead while I'm just sitting here doing nothing. This is a waste of time! How much longer can I sit here? I'm bored. Where's my phone, anyway?*

Relax. Count to ten. Focus on your breathing. Let your mind wander.

There is nothing more important you can do for others than to take care of you. If you are to show up as the person they need, then you must make the time and investment in yourself so you can be that person. They will be grateful you did.

And your future self will be grateful, too.

We have come an incredibly long way. We came into this section understanding purpose—and more importantly our purpose for this time of our life. Now we understand how we grow or improve and the elements of our life that we must consider as we contemplate our purpose.

Now is where the proverbial rubber meets the road. In our last section, it's time to put all of this in action so that we can start experiencing living in a purposeful way.

PART 6:

APPLICATION

"I can't stand it to think my life is going
so fast and I'm not really living it."

—Ernest Hemingway, *The Sun Also Rises*

CHAPTER 18

About Balance

CONTEMPLATING THE END OF HIS LIFE, the king takes his son, the prince, on a walk to share wisdom that the prince will need when he takes over and rules the kingdom.

"Everything you see exists together in a delicate balance," he tells his son. "As king, you need to understand that balance and respect all the creatures, from the crawling ant to the leaping antelope."[1]

His son replies, "But, Dad, don't we eat the antelope?"

You may recognize these lines from the Disney classic *The Lion King*. The music stirs and "Circle of Life" plays. All is well in the universe.

The idea of the balance of nature has been around for ages and is so accepted by people as to be almost beyond question. We use it to consider everything from local land use (cutting down those trees will disturb the balance of the local ecosystem) to climate change (we have to allow the planet to heal from human-caused problems and restore balance).

The problem is that it isn't true. Or at least it's unhelpful in understanding how nature really works. Ecologists, environmentalists, and naturalists have left behind the "balance of nature" metaphor because they know that nature isn't in balance but is in fact constantly changing.[2]

Here are some definitions of balance from various sources:

"An even distribution of weight enabling someone or something to remain upright and steady."[3]

"A state of equilibrium or equipoise; equal distribution of weight, amount."[4]

"Stability produced by even distribution of weight on each side of the vertical axis."[5]

An "even distribution of weight." This is what we picture when we think about balance. Two counteracting forces that are perfectly offset so as to create stasis—meaning nothing is moving.

Nothing in nature is in stasis. Whether measured in minutes or centuries, our world is constantly changing. Temperatures get hotter and colder over the course of a day. We have seasons of the year that are warmer and seasons that are colder. Decades are cooler and then warmer. And over the long history of our planet we have had hot periods and ice ages.

It's not just the temperature that changes. The oceans are constantly rising or falling. Plants are growing or dying. Anyone who has ever gardened or just mowed a lawn will tell you that their work is a continual battle against the constant change of nature. Yet even though everything around us is continually changing, we cling to an ideal that our life should stay in a perfect unchanging state of equilibrium. Where did this come from?

Yin and Yang

The idea of balance in life is an old one. While the concept of dualism—that there are two irreducible and opposing elements that make up the universe and therefore the parts of it—can be inferred in many ancient religions and philosophies, the most well-known is the Eastern philosophy of yin and yang. Dating back potentially as far as the seventh century BC, the light and dark of the yin-yang symbol represent complementary yet opposing forces that make up all aspects of life. Yin symbolizes earth, femaleness, darkness, passivity, and absorption. Yang represents the contrasting forces—heaven, maleness, light, activity, and penetration.[6]

The concept of dualism, or yin and yang, has been applied in numerous ways across the centuries and continually gets applied in new ways to updated philosophies. The theory of order and chaos was popularized by works like *Zen and the Art of Motorcycle Maintenance*[7] and has gained popularity again in the twenty-first century. It is the foundational concept behind the idea of work-life balance.

The yin-yang symbol itself is meant to demonstrate both the interdependence and balance between the two. There is no hierarchy—neither side has more value—rather both sides are reliant on the other and must exist in harmony.

The idea that our life should or even could exist in harmony—in perfect, unchanging balance—is one of the most dangerous lies we can believe. This balance doesn't exist. It's not anywhere in any observable way in the world around us nor in anyone's life. Believing that balance is the ideal creates a standard that is unachievable and sets us up for continual frustration and disappointment. Further, it prevents us from the rewards of embracing the true nature of life—its constant change and seasons.

Just like the changing temperatures, we see the ebb and flow of the parts of our life throughout the days of our life. We have times of the day when we are focused on working and other time for ourselves. We have days of the week where we spend more time with friends and family and other days where we have almost no time at all with them. We have times of the year where we spend most of our week working and then weeks where we are on vacation or holiday and spend no time working at all.

Even as we look at the longer seasons of our life, we see that the amount of time and energy we spend on the different parts of life varies.

As adolescents and students, we are focused on relating and learning—making friends and preparing for the future. We are largely focused on developing ourselves and do almost nothing that adds value in a way that could be considered work.

As parents of young children, we are so focused on working and taking care of our family that self-care gets pushed far to the background.

As empty nesters, we have time again to devote to things we enjoy and that feed us. As retirees, we are no longer working and lean into time with ourselves and other relationships.

The nature of being alive is moving. Even at the molecular level, things that are alive are continually moving. The reason everything is constantly changing is because that is the nature of being alive. Dead things don't move. Just like nature, we are continually going through cycles where parts of our life become hotter and other parts colder only to see them change again.

As you consider how to live a life of purpose, start by releasing yourself from the nonexistent concept of equilibrium. Instead, embrace the beautiful, life-giving reality of change.

Embracing the continually changing ebb and flow of your life is to embrace the fact that you are alive. Realizing that there are times in your life—whether measured in hours, days, or years—when you need to overweight the time and energy you spend on your work releases you from the guilt of spending less time in relationships. Understanding that there are times of your life when you should spend more time and energy on relationships releases you from the pressure of always performing at work to maximize your earnings and career progression. Admitting that there are times of life when you need to focus on developing yourself releases you from the falsehood that you should always, constantly, be available to others.

Embracing Change

But more than releasing us from guilt, embracing the seasons of change allows us to maximize our effectiveness in the areas of life that are most in need at that time. Someone once told me that life consists of a season of "learning, earning, and then teaching." Knowing that you are in your productive earning season will help you focus on doing lots of quality work. Realizing you are in your teaching season will help you serve others in the best way possible.

The good news is that there is no danger from not having all parts of your life in perfect balance at any given point in time. But that's not to say there is no danger. Some days it rains and some days the sun shines and plants need both to grow. If it never rains, then the plants will die. Plants can't live on sunshine alone.

If you neglect any part of your life, trouble ensues. People who neglect relationships end up broken and alone. People who neglect their work end up with nothing to eat and nowhere to live. People who neglect themselves end up hating the person they have become and hurting those around them.

Likewise, if you spend too much time and energy in any one part of your life, that brings peril as well. Remember in chapter 13 when we talked about performance? What happens when you keep working the same muscles over and over again and stay in the stress zone for too long? You get injured. Everything else in your life works the same way. If all you ever do is work and never give yourself time to recover, eventually you are going to get hurt. We've all seen this happen—someone works and works until they are so stressed they have a breakdown. But this principle is true for other parts of life as well.

I am convinced that one of the hardest times of life is when parents (especially mothers) have young children. Babies are all consuming. They are completely helpless and must have everything done for them. Caring for a baby leaves time for almost nothing else—even sleep. Caregivers with multiple young children barely have time to breathe, much less think about working or caring for themselves.

I am in awe of any parent who makes the choice to step away from work and raise children. It's one of the most selfless acts there is. They are making the choice to spend nearly all of their time and energy in very particular relationships. The result is that they are walking away from their work—almost certainly the area of their life where they felt like they were contributing. Yes, raising kids is contributing value to society, but it's a very long-term investment and difficult to feel on most days. Because of the around-the-clock nature of the task of raising children, they are also left with little time and resources to invest in themselves and other relationships that feed them.

This environment creates real challenges. A 2012 study of stay-at-home moms was revealing—they are more likely than working moms to report negative emotions such as worry, sadness, stress, anger, and depression. On the flipside, they are less likely to say that they experience positive emotions such as enjoyment or happiness, or to describe themselves as thriving.[8]

I am not trying to discourage anyone from becoming a stay-at-home parent—it's a noble endeavor. But anyone considering it (or currently doing it) needs to realize the challenge they are going to have by being in a situation that is going to make it very difficult to put energy into things that help them feel as if they are contributing and feeding themselves. Be aware of this and have a plan. You don't have to have a job to feel like you are creating value—find some other way of doing it. And you may not have a lot of time to improve yourself, but find something so that you aren't neglected.

Last but not least, you can even create injury by spending too much time on yourself. You've probably never thought of it this way, but all of us have seen it. They are the eternal student. They are always on the next fad, learning the new philosophy, waiting for the perfect job. Worse, every relationship is about them. Their selfish habits make it hard for them to get close to people. To avoid embarrassment, they pre-emptively end friendships by saying things like "I just don't feel like I'm getting what I need from you."

You probably know someone like this. You're probably related to someone like this. They may be currently living in your basement.

Recovery in Life

In chapter 13, when we studied performance, we discovered that the only way to get stronger is to spend some time in the stress zone. If we want to be better at work, we need to work hard and push ourselves to do uncomfortable, difficult things. If we want to be better in our relationships, we need to work hard at them—we need to be willing to have the hard discussions and do the work of learning about and serving those we are in a relationship with. If we want to be better as a person, we must do the hard work of challenging ourselves. We must struggle with the humility necessary to see ourselves as we really are. We must allow ourselves to be open to different ideas and philosophies from the ones we think are true. We must be open to change.

Those things are hard. And we can't overdo them—we can only take so much hard at any one time. Just like athletes, we need to recover. But how do we do that in life? I have some great news for you there. But first, a short story to illustrate.

Many years ago, when I first started running, I quickly began to have knee problems. It got so bad that I couldn't run anymore. I went to an orthopedic surgeon who determined that there was nothing structurally wrong and so he referred me to a physical therapist.

At my first session, the therapist did a quick examination, showed me a few exercises to do, and then left me with the equipment to go see other patients. I started to do the exercises and quickly began to get frustrated. Not because they were hard, but because none of them involved my knee. Mostly, he had me working my abs and hip muscles.

I looked around and saw that he was working with multiple patients at the same time. Realizing what was happening, I began to get angry. This guy was working with several patients at once so that he could bill for as many people as possible. He was in such a hurry that he didn't even listen to what was wrong with me—he just gave me a list of exercises so he could move on. I was in pain and he was wasting my time!

Finally, he came back around to check on me. "How's it going?" he asked.

"Not well, actually," I replied, trying to control the anger in my voice.

"Oh, what's wrong?"

"Well, I'm not sure you heard me earlier. My problem is with my knees. You gave me a bunch of exercises for my abs and hips."

"Yeah, that's right," he said. "You see the problem isn't with your knees. The problem is with your hips and abs. You use those muscles to power your legs when you run. Because they are weak, they get tired quickly and you start recruiting other muscles in your legs to compensate and that hurts your knees. The way to fix your knees is to make the other muscles in your body stronger."

Athletes have learned that putting too much focus on one body part leads to overdeveloped muscles in that area and weakness in other body parts. And that leads to injuries. Often the answer to recovering from overworking one area of the body is to work another.

Think of each part of your life as a group of muscles. You have work muscles. You can strengthen them through stress and get better at creating value. You have relationship muscles. You can strengthen them and have better relationships. And you even have self muscles. You can strengthen them and become a better person.

Here's the good news. Like strengthening the hips helps the knees, the things that strengthen you in one area of your life provide recovery for another area of your life.

Are you stressed from too much work? How about spending some quality time with other important people in your life? Would spending some time alone doing something you love help?

Are you worn down because you are having to spend all of your time dealing with a difficult relationship? Wouldn't it help to be with someone who encourages you? Or how about just a little distraction of tackling a project?

Are you struggling with illness or pain and tired of doing nothing but going to doctors and fielding questions from people about how you're doing? Doesn't it sound good to just hang with friends who make you laugh? Or to do some work whose return is out in the future—a future that you hope to see?

There is symbiosis in life. Getting stronger at work, relationships, or as an individual makes you better at the other two.

To be a better spouse, father, or friend, I need to be a better person. To be a better person, I need to feel like I am adding value to the world. To truly add value to the world, I need rich relationships with people who will help me.

There is something about seeing my life this way that has changed my perspective on the things I choose to do. I no longer feel the pressure of trying to be perfectly balanced in every part of my life all the time. I accept and even plan for times when I will focus more on one bucket than the other. But I realize that to get better in one area requires that I also continually work on the other two.

What does it actually look like to do the hard work of improving in each area of our life? What are the things we really need to do? That's what each of us must figure out.

CHAPTER 19

About the Plan

I HAVE LEARNED THAT there are generally two reasons people don't embrace purposeful living. The first is that the whole concept seems too esoteric to be understandable. They don't feel that they can possibly understand the meaning of life or our purpose here, and to do so is a waste of time. There is no reason to try. They will simply keep trying to enjoy life and let the chips fall where they may.

The second reason is that they get overwhelmed. They embrace and maybe even understand their purpose. It is meaningful to them, and they wish they could live purposely. A purposeful life seems especially attractive compared to their current life, which feels somewhat meaningless.

The problem is that the idea of living purposely seems to end up competing with reality. I have too many responsibilities and too many things on my plate, so I can't spend time with my family. I must stay in the soul-crushing job because I have to pay my mortgage. I don't have time for exercise when I am always in the car shuttling kids around.

You have now nearly read the entirety of this book, which I hope means you have gotten past the problem of not understanding purpose. Certainly, there are depths we can go to when contemplating our purpose, but really, it's not that complex. Purpose is simply how I live my most joyful life. It's knowing what gives me joy and making choices accordingly. There is no need to overcomplicate it.

Before we end, we need to tackle the problem of being overwhelmed by the prospect of living purposely amid the practical demands of life.

We have a gym on our company campus with trainers who lead individuals through exercise plans to help them achieve goals like losing weight or getting stronger. I worked with one of these trainers for several years who was a complete sadist who liked to watch me suffer. But I'm weird so I loved it and her.

One day I went into the gym for a workout but was stopped as I saw a man who worked at the company lying on the floor with a crowd gathered around him. I located the gym manager and asked her what happened.

"He was working with one of the trainers and passed out."

It is important to understand that this man was what is referred to as a "de-conditioned athlete." That's a nice way of saying he was grossly overweight and out of shape. I also happened to know that he smoked and drank too much and was pushing sixty.

Worried about him, his co-workers had pressed him for months to make changes to his lifestyle. They had gone in together to buy him a package of sessions with an individual trainer to help jumpstart some healthy habits. This was only his second session.

After the paramedics determined he was okay and he went to the locker room to clean up, I began asking the manager and others for more information about what had occurred. I wasn't getting many details. Finally, someone told me that he had collapsed after doing a session of plyometrics.

In case you don't know what that is, Harvard Health describes plyometrics as involving "short, intense bursts of activity that target fast-twitch muscle fibers in the lower body. These fibers help generate explosive power that increases speed and jumping height."[1] Have you ever seen someone jumping up and down on those tall boxes in the corner of the gym? That's plyometrics. There is probably no exercise that gets your heart rate up as quickly as plyometrics.

You may be thinking to yourself, "That doesn't sound like an exercise that an overweight, out-of-shape sixty-year-old man who smokes should be doing."

You would be correct.

The people who know me will tell you that I rarely get mad. It takes a lot for me to display anger. But after I heard that . . .

I was livid.

Someone who is supposed to know better put this man in danger. It was more than irresponsible; it was borderline abusive. "His goal right now should be to be able to walk on a treadmill for twenty minutes, not jump up on plyometric boxes! That is hard even for top athletes!"

Not surprising, to my knowledge that man never set foot in the gym again. The experience affirmed what he thought—that getting in shape was so hard as to be insurmountable. He was too far gone to be able to get back into a healthy condition. If he passed out in only his second workout, he didn't have any chance of going further. He went right back to his unhealthy lifestyle.

Any of us can look at that situation and see the folly of someone who isn't prepared jumping into an advanced workout routine. Yet, we do the same thing to ourselves when we think that living a purposeful life means that we suddenly become Gandhi overnight. Not even Gandhi became Gandhi overnight.

Learning to Trust Yourself

New Year's resolutions are notoriously useless. One study said that only 9 percent of adults keep their resolutions all year, and 23 percent abandon them in the first week.[2] I have no idea if this is right, but it certainly feels plausible.

I love to ask people about their New Year's resolutions. Some of them are inspiring and I copy them. But some of them (and I apologize if I offend you) are downright ridiculous.

"I'm going to run a marathon this year!"

"Have you ever run a 5K before?"

"Nope."

Good luck with that.

"This year, I'm going to get debt free!"

"Is your paycheck more than your debt payments?"

"Nope."

Uh huh.

It's no wonder that we don't think we can live purposely. All the things we associate with purposeful living—great relationships, self-discipline, peace of mind, achievement—are so beyond us that when we try it's embarrassing.

Here's my favorite. This is the summary of an actual conversation I had with someone a few years ago.

"Did you make New Year's resolutions?"

"Yes, but I know I won't do them."

"Then why did you make them?"

"I like having goals."

Wow.

One of the most important traits we can develop is trust in ourselves. When we regularly make promises to ourselves and keep them, we begin to develop the confidence we need to set bigger and bigger goals. If I can't trust myself to do small things, then I can't trust myself to do big things. When I regularly set and achieve my goals, then I start to believe I am someone who does what they say they will do. That gives me the confidence to take the risk of setting bigger goals.

This isn't just about starting small. It's about learning the value of compounding.

There is a statement that's often attributed to Albert Einstein: "Compound interest is the most powerful force in the universe."

Now, it's doubtful that Einstein really said that, but whoever did was onto something.

Let's say you borrow $10,000 with an interest rate of a mere 1 percent per month. That means the first month you are only charged $100 interest so now you owe $10,100. That doesn't sound too bad. Then the next month you are charged interest on the $100 also, so the second month interest is $101 with a balance of $10,201. Only one dollar more—no big deal.

After a year, you look at your statement and see that you owe $11,156.68 and were charged $110.46 in interest that month. Huh. That's 10 percent more than you paid the first month. Still doable, I guess.

Because it feels so small, you forget about the loan for a while until five years later and you get a notice in the mail saying that the loan is coming due, and you now owe $20,268 and are being charged more than $200 a month in interest.

Wait a minute. I thought this was only charging me $100 a month in interest? How did it double?

That's compound interest. Small amounts multiplied by small amounts grow to big amounts over time. Compound interest can be painful for the borrower, but it can be wonderful for the lender. The small, purposeful actions that you implement in your life compound. They don't just add to your life, they multiply.

Living purposely isn't going from the couch to a marathon, it's starting by taking the stairs. And then pretty soon you are strong enough to walk a trail. And then run a mile. Then five miles. Then twenty-six.

Every step allows you to experience the rewards of purposeful living, which not only makes you want to do more, but also makes you aware of what else you can do.

If your relationship with your spouse is struggling, there is no magic wand you can wave and suddenly become healthy again. But you can start doing something small like putting down the cell phone and simply listening. After a while, when your partner starts to feel heard, you can start engaging in deeper conversations.

If you have been stuck in a job that you don't enjoy and could do in your sleep, you're probably not going to be able to change to a new dream job overnight. But you can start taking courses to learn new skills that will open other opportunities.

If you feel called to address the plight of at-risk children, you aren't going to be able to save them all in one day. But you can get involved in the life of one child, which may help you understand how to help even more children.

Wherever you decide to focus, the point is just to get going. There is an old saying in business that "activity brings activity." The idea is that the more you are doing, the more likely you are to find things to do. Pick up the phone and call someone. Send an email. Do some research. Visit a friend. Pick something small and achievable to start with and let it snowball from there.

Putting It in Action

Here is where we get down to details. If you are going to get better at living purposely, you must have a plan that will help you bring your unconscious actions to your conscious. To start making purposeful decisions requires that you do things on purpose. This means you will need to make some changes to change the inertia of your habits and the whirlwind of your life. To pull off something like that, you need a plan.

Step 1: What makes me stronger?

Look at your mantra and all the things you wrote down in chapter 11. Now think about each bucket—Work, Relationships, Self—and ask yourself:

Given my purpose—the experience I want to have in life—what are the things I can do that will make me stronger in this area? What can I do to better be able to contribute and add value to the world? Maybe it's learning a new skill, getting a degree, finding somewhere to volunteer, or raising your hand to take on a new project at work.

What can I do to improve my relationships? Make sure you consider all relationships that are important to you—family, friends, spouse, and even your network. Maybe it's taking my spouse out for a monthly dinner, phoning my mother once a week, or scheduling a getaway with my college friends.

What can I do to feed my soul and become a better person? Maybe it's deciding to take the stairs instead of the elevator at work, reading a book instead of watching TV, scheduling ten minutes for a morning meditation, or only drinking alcohol one day a week. Maybe it's committing to train for a triathlon!

Keep in mind that this is the brainstorming part of the exercise—which means that creativity is the goal, not criticism. Don't (yet) listen to the part of the brain that says, "You can't do that," or "You don't have time for that." We'll get there. For now, just try to think of small things that you can start with as well as big things that may serve as long-term inspirations.

Step 2: What should I eliminate?

Now that you have all these ideas of things you could be doing, let's take a look at what you are actually doing now by taking an inventory of how you spend your time.

There are 8,760 hours in a year (and 24 more in a leap year).

Assuming you sleep 8 hours per night (and if you don't you should), that means you are awake for 5,840 hours per year.

If you have a job where you work 40 hours per week and take three weeks of vacation, that's 1,960 work hours, leaving you awake and not working for 3,880 hours per year.

What do you do with all those hours?

The average American spends one hour commuting to their job each workday[3] (245 hours per year) and one hour eating per day[4] (365 hours per year). Then there are chores. Americans spend on average eighteen hours a week on errands and housework.[5] That's 936 hours per year shopping, cooking, and cleaning. We also spend about an hour per day showering, brushing our teeth, and performing other personal hygiene tasks[6]—so that's another 365 hours per year.

So after we've done our job, gone to the grocery store, made dinner, cleaned the house, finally taken a shower, and gotten a full 8 hours of sleep—all the things we "have to" do—we have 1,969 hours left. That's more than five hours per day at our complete discretion.

Now, my guess is at this point you are going back to check my math because you certainly don't feel like you have a free five hours a day.

So maybe you work more than forty hours a week, and maybe your kitchen is spotless because you clean constantly, and maybe you are driving kids to practices and recitals at all hours. But the harsh reality is that, as we said in chapter 2, those are choices. No one is forcing you to work overtime. You could choose to not have your son play baseball.

Do your own math. Look at your calendar and think about what you are actually doing with your time. But let me give you a tip on one place to look you may have forgotten.

Using our American averages, we determined that people in our country have about five hours per day of discretionary time after they finish all their have-tos. Want to guess how much time the average American spends each day consuming media (mass or social)?

Eight hours per day.[7] Which I suppose means we are looking at our phones when we are eating, driving, and showering.

I don't want to depress you, but if you are brutally honest about how much time you spend watching TV or scrolling on your phone, you may be shocked.

So here is my question: Whatever things you listed that fill up your discretionary time, which of them are you willing to give up so that you can replace it with something on your purpose list?

Are you willing to stream one less show and spend thirty minutes a day reading? How about committing to just one day a week with no social media so you can use that time to check in with friends? Instead of the hour you spend in bed each night playing games on your phone, how about getting up thirty minutes earlier so you can get in that workout?

Here's another way to think about your time: What things are you doing that make you *weaker* in an area of your life? We came up with a list of things that could make us stronger, but what are we doing that is actually harming us? Things we do that are harming our relationships, making us less effective in our jobs, or damaging our body? What are we doing that we are going to regret?

If you are going to say yes to one thing, it means you are going to say no to something else.

What are you willing to say no to?

Step 3: Consider the Whole Picture

Before we finalize our plan, let's first make sure we've considered our time from a different perspective.

Most people think of hunter-gatherer societies as constantly working to find food, with no time to devote to anything beyond mere survival. It turns out this isn't true. Humans are good at

coordinating their efforts in ways that develop surplus food supplies to allow members of a group to specialize in other functions.[8]

Dr. Bethany Turner is an anthropologist at Georgia State
University. She has an immense understanding of ancient civilizations. According to Dr. Turner, hunter-gatherers "had the
equivalent of part-time jobs getting food, and then the rest of
the time was leisure time."[9] But they didn't think of leisure the
way we do.

Dr. Turner notes that typically in twenty-first-century Western
societies, we think of leisure time as doing nothing or being lazy.
But that's not the only way to think about leisure. Leisure is simply
what you do when you aren't working. Dr. Turner asks, what about
sitting around telling stories? She told me:

> If leisure includes storytelling, there are oral traditions
> among indigenous peoples in various parts of the world
> that appear to accurately map the landscape going back
> seven thousand years that contain stunning amounts
> of accumulated knowledge. Sitting around and telling
> stories? That may be leisure time but it's foundationally
> important to human culture.

But these egalitarian societies weren't just sitting around while
they told stories; it was woven into their routine. Turner continued:

> Sharing of resources, knowledge, techniques—there
> wouldn't be a formalized educational system where you
> gather all the children together and someone lectures
> them about the best way to make a particular tool.
> The children would be engaging in imitative behavior
> while the adults are potentially sitting around gossiping
> and telling stories and are also maintaining tools and
> repairing clothing.

Driving a child to soccer practice may not feel all that important, but it can be purposeful. That time in the car may be the one time you can ask your child a question that will get him to open up.

When my kids were young, my wife and I were committed to having dinner together as a family as often as possible. While there is value in simply eating together, for us that wasn't enough. We purposely used that time to ask questions and talk with our kids about all kinds of topics that were often beyond what they would normally be thinking about. It was organic—nothing formalized or awkward. Often, it was just telling them stories about things happening in our world in ways they could understand. We loved being together but always looked for ways of making that time even more purposeful.

Living purposely requires saying no to things that go against your purpose and saying yes to purposeful activities. But it also means seeing the potential for purpose in everything we do—even the so-called have-tos.

There are no hard lines between the buckets of life. Look for activities that allow you to get stronger in multiple areas at once. Develop rewarding relationships with people you work with. Find relationships that help you become a better person. Learn personal skills that are transferable to your job.

Seek out the most valuable activities you can. If you have positive people in your life who encourage and strengthen you as a person, be purposeful about spending more time with them. Pick a book to read with your spouse so you can talk about it and grow together. Develop the habit of asking yourself the question, "Is there anything I can do to make this moment more purposeful?"

Before you move on, pause to consider what you are doing today. Is there anything you are currently doing that you not only want to keep doing, but actually want to spend more time and energy doing? Is there an opportunity to add elements of purpose to things you must do?

Step 4: Making Choices

We need to do some prioritizing.

Now that you have a list of potential strengthening activities from Steps 1 and 3, determine how much time each action would take. If you listed that you could work out for thirty minutes four days per week, that's two hours per week. If you thought about mentoring an at-risk child, that could be two hours per month. If you are trying to build your relationship with your teenage daughter and think it could help to stop by her room every night before she goes to sleep, that's anywhere from thirty seconds to two hours.

Add all the time together. My guess is that doing all those things would take more time than you feel you have to give. That means it's time to make some choices.

Go back through your list of strengthening activities and evaluate them from two perspectives:

First, think about how achievable that activity is. Given your circumstances, limitations, abilities, and resources, how likely are you to be able to complete that activity?

Second, rate how impactful the activity is. If you were to complete it, how significant would the impact be on helping you live your purpose?

The obvious place to start is with activities that are highly achievable and will have a big impact. There may be some things that are hard but would have such a big impact that they are worth the effort. Focus on those before you get to the low-impact items.

Before you make your final choices, remember what we learned in chapter 13 about periodization—how athletes think about training and recovery from a daily, weekly, monthly, and even yearly perspective. Make sure that you have activities that hit each of your buckets in each period. There will be times and seasons of weighting one bucket over the others, but you can't totally ignore a bucket for long. For instance, if your only plan to invest in your marriage is through a yearly one-week vacation, you are not going to have a

healthy marriage. Find little things to do each day or week in addition to the big things that are more seasonal.

Depending on where you are in life, what you choose from your
list will vary. If you have been really focused on work for a while,
all of your items may be in the buckets of relationship and self.
And depending on the intensity of the activities you choose and
how much discretionary time you have, your list may be long or
short. But I do suggest keeping in mind the Power of Three: You
can remember and focus on three things.

So that's it. You've got a list of choices you are going to make to
move you along in your journey of living purposely. You are on your
way to a joy-filled life. Now all you have to do is do it. So simple.

Step 5: Accountability

Nineteenth-century Prussian military commander Helmuth von
Moltke is credited with coining the phrase: "No plan of operations
extends with certainty beyond the first encounter with the enemy's
main force."[10]

Or as Mike Tyson posted on X, "Everyone has a plan till they
get punched in the mouth."

Life likes to punch us in the mouth. Despite great intentions, the
whirlwind of life can distract us from the things we really desire to
do. Here are four things that can help us live our purposeful plan:

1. Step on a pebble

Have you ever gotten a pebble in your shoe? It's so annoying.
You can keep walking, but it hurts and you can't ignore it. I like
to come up with pebbles that I can't ignore to make me conscious
about choices.

For example, let's say you want to spend more time reading, so
you decide that your pebble for reading will be streaming. Every
time you open a video streaming app, ask yourself, "Will I be glad

that I watched this video right now or would I have wished I read a book?" You can certainly choose to binge the new series, but you don't get to do it automatically. You have to answer the question—you must stop to get the pebble out of your shoe.

2. Keep score

Gamification is a trick that a lot of consumer companies use to get you to use more of their product. "If you buy one more coffee this month then you move up to our Gold level!" Figure out what Gold Level membership means for you.

If you decided to work out four times a week, keep track of every time you work out so you have a record and can know if you really did it. If you want to be more present with your partner, put a piece of paper next to your toothbrush and place a check mark for every day you really listened.

Make activity goals as specific and measurable as you can so you know if you did them. Instead of saying "I'm going to eat better," decide that you won't eat any processed foods on at least four days each week. You don't know if you kept a promise to yourself if you don't keep score, and if it's written down it's hard to deny.

3. Socialize your plan

Telling someone your plan is hard to do. It can be humbling and even embarrassing. However, for some of the most difficult things we want to accomplish in life, telling someone is one of the most helpful things we can do.

The hardest part of triathlon training for me was the early morning swims—especially during the winter. There is something about getting out of a warm bed and into a cold pool that is daunting. So swimming was the part of training that I often did with other people. If I wasn't at the pool at 5:30 in the morning to meet them, I'd hear about it. So I got out of that warm bed.

The challenge here is that depending on where you are in life, suddenly announcing to people that you are going to do all these purposeful things may set them back. They may even be more discouraging than helpful. Seek out people who want the best for you and will assist you. And even then, you don't have to give them the whole story.

4. Be fluid

More than anything, remember that this is a journey. There is no way you are going to come up with the perfect plan. And even the perfect plan becomes imperfect when circumstances change.

You set a goal of walking the neighborhood every morning before work. You're doing great until your middle schooler joins the chess club that meets at 7:00 a.m. Well, there goes the walks.

It's the principles of purposeful living that matter more than the practices. Focus on what you are trying to accomplish—your mantra for how to experience the most joyful version of your life. Then celebrate how the seasons and circumstances change how you live it.

CHAPTER 20

About Purpose

"I JUST WANT MORE moments like that."

I listened as my friend, in a moment of great vulnerability and emotion, made this confession to our small group. He had just described what he called a euphoric moment.

"I had just finished a workout and was looking over a beautiful lake. I sat there thinking about how I am really killing it at work. I mean I am just really in my zone. And then I thought about this incredible conversation with my daughter that I had the night before and how strong my relationships are with my kids right now. And I'm at this incredible place with my wife and I, well, I just thought, wow, this is what I feel like my life was meant to be. I just felt so whole. So complete.

"And then I thought, what can I do to feel like this more often? I just want to figure out how to have more moments like that."

Indeed. Don't we all?

I hope you can identify with my friend. I hope you have had moments where you felt that you were doing what you were meant to do. Living the life you were meant to live. Contributing in a way that only you can. Reveling in the richness of a deeply satisfying relationship. Resting in the calm of your nourished soul.

If you've never had an inkling of that feeling, I wish it for you.

We all know that those moments of completeness are so desirous because they are so rare. Momentary glimpses of heaven amaze us because often it seems we are living in hell. The default state of the world is cruel and hard. Our nature is to seek the satisfaction of fleeting pleasures that almost always result in pain for those around us. Not knowing how to cure our pain, we mask it through a continual series of temporary fixes—fleeting moments of escape that just make things worse. Even when we want to change, to pursue something different, better, or more lasting, we continually get dragged back into the morass of a world intent on including us in its misery.

The gravitational pull of the way of living espoused by the world is massive. We are bombarded by messages promising us happiness if we would only buy this or consume that, only to find an emptiness that yields nothing but a constant craving for more. We are fed a constant stream of lies that promise security yet pit us against each other and only drive us further into isolation.

Amid all of this, how can we possibly focus our attention on things that can lead us to something better?

If we are going to overcome the incredible distractions of this world, we must have something pulling us that is more powerful than the things holding us back. There must be a version of life that is so desirous that it overcomes our unconscious desire for pleasure and comfort and all the things the world is telling us that we ought to do.

David Brooks addresses this well: "If you want to win the war for attention, don't try to say 'no' to the trivial distractions . . . try to say 'yes' to the subject that arouses a terrifying longing, and let the terrifying longing crowd out everything else."[1]

What arouses a terrifying longing in you? What do you desire that is so attractive that it can pull you away from all the things that are competing for your attention?

We started this book with a sobering exploration of death, because understanding the temporal nature of our existence is powerful in setting the context of our life. Let's finish by considering death one more time.

There is a sentence in the Bible that is as difficult as it is powerful: "The day of death is better than the day of birth."[2]

How can this be? The day a baby is born is a cause for celebration, while the day someone dies causes mourning. How can someone possibly claim that the day someone dies is better than when they are born?

Let's go back to minister and author David Gibson to explain:

> The day of death is better than the day of birth—not because death is better than life; it's not—but because a coffin is a better preacher than a cot. When life ends, or is about to end, absolutely everything else comes into focus. The things that don't really matter, but which we gave so much time to, now seem so empty and pointless. The lives we touched and the generosity we showed and the love we gave or received now mean so much more.[3]

The day of our death is one of life's best teachers. We celebrate birth as a time of hope and renewal, but there is nothing to be learned from it compared to when we die. Viewing our life through our death instructs us on how to live. Knowing that our life is brief with both our joys and struggles lasting but a moment, creates a vivid awareness that our chance to enjoy life happens today.

Our society has become fanatical about living longer. The amount of information available regarding how to extend length and quality of life is incredible. There are constant reports about new technology to help us live longer and better. Genetic modification, brain implants, and artificial organs are but a few of the technologies that are seemingly around the corner in helping us live long and well.

Once I was at a presentation by someone who wanted to help people figure out a plan to live to their desired age. He was asking the people in the group to state a number for how long they wanted to live. People answered: "85!"; "100!"; or "125!" He came to me, and I demurred.

"I'd rather not answer—go on to the next person."

He pressed, trying to get me to say something. It got awkward so I finally answered. "I find the question unhelpful and even dangerous."

Now it was really awkward.

Fixating on the future in a futile attempt to live to a certain age—something I can't control—distracts me from the only thing I can control—how I live today. I might live to be one hundred, but I also may get hit by a car tomorrow. I want to live so that whenever my last day is, whether it is in fifty years or this week, my last days are as joy-filled as they can be.

What terrifies me is wasting one day on anything less than the best of what life has to offer. Once you realize how good life can be when you are living purposely—focused on others and consciously choosing joy regardless of circumstances—it makes every other version of life pale in comparison. The idea of experiencing anything else is indeed terrifying.

One Final Encouragement

My chest was tight, and my breathing constricted. My head began to hurt from the immense tension in my neck and shoulders.

Luckily, I had the awareness to recognize the physical symptoms of incredible stress. I got up from behind my desk and walked over to a couch across the room and led myself through some meditative breathing exercises. I needed to get my heart rate down and my head clear so I could think again.

It was the summer of 2020, a time of incredible challenge for everyone. As a leader of a healthcare company, I was facing some unique pressures. COVID hotspots were beginning to pop up around the country, and any hope for a quick resolution was fading as we began to face the reality of a prolonged pandemic.

One particular problem for our business was the ongoing elimination of elective surgeries. Surgery is a significant part of what we do, and we had been holding on as best we could in the hope they would restart. As the crisis worsened over the summer, it seemed that many operating rooms weren't going to reopen any time soon.

This meant I was faced with the decision of doing a significant layoff for the first time in our company's twenty-year history. The livelihood of hundreds of people was at stake as I considered how to keep the company afloat and protect the thousands of others who depended on us. It was a massive burden.

Concurrently, like every other parent of school-aged children in the country, my wife and I were faced with the decision of what to do about our children's school that fall. In our area, many schools were giving the option of in-person or virtual. Having witnessed the futile efforts at virtual schooling that spring, we felt great concern about the quality of virtual education and a conviction that in-person learning would be far superior. Not to mention the social and psychological challenges associated with kids who are locked up in their rooms all day and isolated from friends.

However, there was still so little known about the virus and so much concern about the damage it could do. Complicating things for us, our daughter, who was moving into high school as a freshman, had begun to have severe health issues over the past year, which no doctor had been able to diagnose. With the lockdowns of that spring, our access to her doctors had all but been eliminated and we had no idea of the risk that the virus posed to her.

My decisions about the layoff of my colleagues and school for my children were both coming to a head at the same time, and the weight of those decisions began to have a physical impact on me. As I sat there trying to focus on my breathing, I thought to myself, "Not only do I not know what to do, I don't even know how to think about figuring out what to do."

What's the template? What are the questions to ask? How do I even think about what decisions to make?

In that moment, the only thing I could do was go back to the teachings that were foundational in my life. As I thought about my most treasured values and my most deeply held beliefs, I realized that those were the things that had always driven my decisions. The question I needed to be asking wasn't regarding what principles should drive these decisions. The question was whether the principles that drive my decisions are from a source that is to be trusted.

As you can probably tell from reading this book, I have spent years exploring and studying many different sources looking for wisdom. I have found helpful guidance from many places. There is much to be learned from so many different philosophies.

Your Beliefs

In the end, I have continually come back to the teachings of Jesus. The more I have studied his life and teaching, the more I have seen how truly counter they are to what the world tells us. And more importantly, how truly incredible the life is that results from following those teachings. Virtually every concept in this book owes its source to His words.

I am not trying to convince you to believe in any specific religion— the aim of this book is not to cause you to become a Christian.

However, I do want to convince you that before setting off on this journey of purposeful living, it is vital to take the time to think about where your core beliefs came from. Ask yourself if the source of your beliefs is to be trusted. Is what is setting the aim of your life based on something that is true and truly wants the best for you? Have your actions that have been driven by those beliefs resulted in the kind of life you want?

I also want to convince you to continually ask those questions. Allow yourself the freedom to reevaluate your beliefs with the assurance that if they are true then they can withstand any challenge. The more often you delve into a search for truth, the more likely you are to find it.

Our life is finite. We only get one shot at it. After today is done, it is gone. It is to be savored because it is so brief. It is to be enjoyed because there is nothing else to enjoy.

See your inevitable struggles as signs that you are progressing on your journey. Let the pain of life serve to energize you as a reminder of how wonderful purposeful living is by comparison.

You are empowered. You are equipped. You are ready.

Don't settle for anything less than the best of what life has to offer.

Acknowledgments

WRITING A BOOK IS HARD AND TAKES A LOT OF TIME. It is especially difficult when you are also running a healthcare business coming out of a global pandemic. I could not have done this without my incredible team who keeps our company improving the lives of everyone we touch—even when I'm tucked away somewhere writing. I specifically want to thank Anne Patton, Lisa Lilienthal, and Robyn Melhuish for your incredible work in making the vision of this book a reality.

Notes

Chapter 1

1. James 4:14. New International Version.
2. David Gibson, *Living Life Backward: How Ecclesiastes Teaches Us to Live in Light of the End* (Wheaton, IL: Crossway, 2017).

Chapter 2

1. Tejvan Pettinger, "Facts About Global Poverty," *Economics Help*, October 18, 2020, https://www.economicshelp.org/blog/147866/economics/facts-about-global-poverty/.
2. Angel E. Navidad, "Stanford Marshmallow Test Experiment," *Simply Psychology*, last modified September 7, 2023, https://www.simplypsychology.org/marshmallow-test.html.
3. Navidad, "Stanford Marshmallow Test Experiment."
4. Oliver Burkeman, *Four Thousand Weeks: Time Management for Mortals* (New York: Farrar, Straus and Giroux, 2021), 61.

Chapter 3

1. Viktor E. Frankl, *Man's Search for Meaning* (Boston: Beacon Press, 2006), 66.

2. Frankl, *Man's Search for Meaning*, 101.

Chapter 4

1. The Presbytery of the United States, Free Church of Scotland (Continuing), "The Westminster Shorter Catechism," accessed May 2024, https://www.westminsterconfession.org/resources/confessional-standards/the-westminster-shorter-catechism/.

Chapter 7

1. Constantine Sedikides and John J. Skowronski, "In Human Memory, Good Can Be Stronger Than Bad," *Association for Psychological Science* 29, no. 1 (2020): 86–91, https://journals.sagepub.com/doi/pdf/10.1177/0963721419896363.

2. Viktor E. Frankl, *Man's Search for Meaning* (Boston: Beacon Press, 2006), 133.

3. Learn more at https://www.ytfoundation.org.

4. Jeffrey Sullivan, Julia Thornton Snider, Emma van Eijndhoven, Tony Okoro, Katherine Batt, and Thomas Deleir, "The Well-Being of Long-Term Cancer Survivors," *The American Journal of Managed Care* 24, no. 4 (April 2018): 188–195, https://pubmed.ncbi.nlm.nih.gov/29668209/.

5. Sullivan et al., "The Well-Being of Long-Term Cancer Survivors."

6. Arthur Brooks, *From Strength to Strength: Finding Success, Happiness, and Deep Purpose in the Second Half of Life* (New York: Portfolio/Penguin, 2022), 89.

Chapter 8

1. Imed Bouchrika, PhD, "College Dropout Rates: 2024 Statistics by Race, Gender & Income," Research.com, April 17, 2024, https://research.com/universities-colleges/college-dropout-rates.

2. Melanie Hanson, "College Dropout Rates," Education Data Initiative, last updated October 29, 2023, https://educationdata.org/college-dropout-rates.

3. NCHEMS Information Center, "Difference in Median Earnings Between High School Diploma and a Bachelors Degree," 2010, http://www.higheredinfo.org/dbrowser/index.php?submeasure=366&year=2010&level=nation&mode=data&state=.

4. Mike Brown, "College Dropouts and Student Debt," LendEDU, November 2, 2017, https://lendedu.com/blog/college-dropouts-student-loan-debt/.

5. Carolyn Facteau (Executive Coach) in discussion with the author on June 15, 2023. All subsequent quotes are taken from the same interview.

Chapter 10

1. Arthur Brooks, *From Strength to Strength: Finding Success, Happiness, and Deep Purpose in the Second Half of Life* (New York: Portfolio/Penguin, 2022), 26–27.

Chapter 13

1. Scottie Parker in discussion with the author on August 31, 2023. All subsequent quotes are taken from the same interview.

Chapter 14

1. Siva Raja and Sharon L. Stein, "Work-Life Balance: History, Costs, and Budgeting for Balance," *Clinics in Colon and Rectal Surgery* 27, no. 2 (June 2014): 71–74, https://www.ncbi.nlm.nih.gov/pmc/articles/PMC4079063/.

2. Shawn M. Carter, "Work Life Balance Outranks an Easy Commute and Paths to Promotion in Employee Values, New Survey Finds," *Forbes*, May 13, 2022, https://www.forbes.com/health/mind/work-life-balance-survey/.

3. Charlie Giattino, Esteban Ortiz-Ospina, and Max Roser, "Working Hours," Our World in Data, 2020, https://ourworldindata.org/working-hours.

Chapter 15

1. Saloni Dattani, Lucas Rodés-Guirao, Hannah Ritchie, MaEsteban Ortiz-Ospina, and Max Roser, "Life Expectancy," Our World in Data, 2023, https://ourworldindata.org/life-expectancy.

2. Saloni Dattani, Fiona Spooner, Hannah Ritchie, and Max Roser, "Child and Infant Mortality," Our World in Data, 2023, https://ourworldindata.org/child-mortality.

3. Sharon Basraba, "Life Expectancy from Prehistory to 1800 and Beyond," *Verywell Health*, last updated June 23, 2023, https://www.verywellhealth.com/longevity-throughout-history-2224054.

4. Dora L. Costa, *The Evolution of Retirement: An American Economic History, 1880–1990* (Chicago: University of Chicago Press, 1998).

5. Costa, *The Evolution of Retirement.*

6. Linh Dang, Aparna Ananthasubramaniam, and Briana Mezuk, "Spotlight on the Challenges of Depression following Retirement and Opportunities for Interventions," *Clinical Interventions in Aging* 17 (July 7, 2022): 1037–1056, https://doi.org/10.2147/CIA.S336301.

7. National Institute of Mental Health, "Major Depression," last updated July 2023, https://www.nimh.nih.gov/health/statistics/major-depression.

8. George Jerjian, "A 67-year-old who 'un-retired' shares the biggest retirement challenge that 'no one talks about,'" *CNBC Make It*, June 15, 2022, https://www.cnbc.com/2022/06/15/67-year-old-who-unretired-at-62-shares-the-biggest-retirement-challenge-that-no-one-talks-about.html.

9. Edward Jones, "Longevity and the New Journey of Retirement: An Edward Jones and Age Wave Study," May 2022, 16, https://www.edwardjones.com/sites/default/files/acquiadam/2022-05/AgeWaveReportMay2022.pdf.

10. Richard Fry and Dana Braga, "The Growth of the Older Workforce," Pew Research Center, December 14, 2023, https://www.pewresearch.org/social-trends/2023/12/14/the-growth-of-the-older-workforce/.

11. Eric S. Kim, Ashley V. Whillans, Matthew T. Lee, Ying Chen, Tyler J. VanderWeele, "Volunteering and Subsequent Health and Well-Being in Older Adults: An Outcome-Wide Longitudinal Approach," *American Journal of Preventive Medicine* 59, no. 2 (Aug 2020): 176–186, https://www.ncbi.nlm.nih.gov/pmc/articles/PMC7375895/.

12. Bob Buford, *Halftime: Moving from Success to Significance* (Grand Rapids, MI: Zondervan, 1994), 83–85.

Chapter 16

1. Liz Mineo, "Good Genes Are Nice but Joy Is Better," *The Harvard Gazette*, April 11, 2017, https://news.harvard.edu/gazette/story/2017/04/over-nearly-80-years-harvard-study-has-been-showing-how-to-live-a-healthy-and-happy-life/.

2. Joshua Wolf Shenk, "What Makes Us Happy?" *The Atlantic*, June 2009, https://www.theatlantic.com/magazine/archive/2009/06/what-makes-us-happy/307439/.

3. George E. Vaillant, MD, *Aging Well: Surprising Guideposts to a Happier Life from the Landmark Study of Adult Development* (New York: Little, Brown Spark, 2002).

4. Robert Waldinger, MD, "What Makes a Good Life? Lessons from the Longest Running Study on Happiness," TED Talk, 2015, https://www.youtube.com/watch?v=8KkKuTCFvzI, cited in Mineo, "Good Genes Are Nice but Joy is Better."

5. Waldinger, "What Makes a Good Life?"

6. Mineo, "Good Genes Are Nice but Joy Is Better."

7. National Academies of Sciences, Engineering, and Medicine, *Social Isolation and Loneliness in Older Adults: Opportunities for the Health Care System* (Washington, DC: The National Academies Press, 2020), https://doi.org/10.17226/25663.

8. National Academies of Sciences, Engineering, and Medicine, *Social Isolation*.

9. Genesis 2:18. English Standard Version.

10. National Foster Youth Institute, "51 Useful Aging Out of Foster Care Statistics," accessed May 2024, https://nfyi.org/51-useful-aging-out-of-foster-care-statistics-social-race-media/.

11. Lydia Denworth, *Friendship: The Evolution, Biology, and Extraordinary Power of Life's Fundamental Bond* (New York: W.W. Norton, 2020), 80.

12. Denworth, *Friendship*, 7.

13. Denworth, *Friendship*, 81.

14. Kira M. Newman, "Why Your Friends Are More Important Than You Think," *Greater Good Magazine*, July 7, 2020, https://greatergood.berkeley.edu/article/item/why_your_friends_are_more_important_than_you_think.

15. Denworth, *Friendship*, 153.

16. W. Bradford Wilcox, Wendy Wang, "Who Is Happiest? Married Mothers and Fathers, Per the Latest General Social Survey," Institute for Family Studies, September 12, 2023, https://ifstudies.org/blog/who-is-happiest-married-mothers-and-fathers-per-the-latest-general-social-survey.

17. Denworth, *Friendship*, 248.

Chapter 17

1. John LaRosa, "Self-Improvement Market Recovers from the Pandemic, Worth $13.4 Billion in the U.S.," *Market Research Blog*, September 2023, https://blog.marketresearch.com/self-improvement-market-recovers-from-the-pandemic-worth-13.4-billion-in-the-u.s.

2. Hsin-Yu An, Wei Chen, Cheng-Wei Wang, Hui-Fei Yang, Wan-Ting Huang, and Sheng-Yu Fan, "The Relationships between Physical Activity and Life Satisfaction and Happiness among Young, Middle-Aged, and Older Adults," *International Journal of Environmental Research and Public Health* 17, no. 13 (2020): 4817, https://doi.org/10.3390/ijerph17134817.

3. Peter Attia, *Outlive: The Science and Art of Longevity* (New York: Harmony/Crown, 2023), 17.

4. Matthew J. Zawadzki, Joshua M. Smyth, and Heather J. Costigan, "Real-Time Associations Between Engaging in Leisure and Daily Health and Well-Being," *Annals of Behavioral Medicine: A Publication of the Society of Behavioral Medicine* 49, no. 4 (August 2015), https://pubmed.ncbi.nlm.nih.gov/25724635/.

5. C. S. Lewis, *Mere Christianity* (Digital Edition, HarperCollins e-books, 2021).

6. Lydia Denworth, *Friendship: The Evolution, Biology, and Extraordinary Power of Life's Fundamental Bond* (New York: W.W. Norton, 2020), 78.

Chapter 18

1. *The Lion King*, directed by Roger Allers and Rob Minkoff (United States: Buena Vista Pictures, 1994).

2. Tik Root, "The 'Balance of Nature' Is an Enduring Concept. But It's Wrong." *National Geographic*, July 26, 2019, https://www.nationalgeographic.com/environment/article/balance-of-nature-explained.

3. Oxford Languages, s.v. "balance," accessed May 9, 2024, https://www.google.com/search?q=balance.

4. Dictionary.com, s.v. "balance," accessed May 9, 2024, https://www.dictionary.com/browse/balance.

5. *Merriam Webster*, s.v. "balance," accessed May 9, 2024, https://www.merriam-webster.com/dictionary/balance.

6. *Encyclopedia Britannica*, s.v. "yinyang," accessed February 12, 2024, https://www.britannica.com/topic/yinyang.

7. Robert M. Pirsig, *Zen and the Art of Motorcycle Maintenance* (New York: William Morrow, 1974).

8. Elizabeth Mendes, Lydia Saad, and Kyley McGeeney, "Stay-at-Home Moms Report More Depression, Sadness, Anger," Gallup News, May 18, 2012, https://news.gallup.com/poll/154685/stay-home-moms-report-depression-sadness-anger.aspx.

Chapter 19

1. Matthew Solan, "Plyometrics: Three Explosive Exercises Even Beginners Can Try," Harvard Health Publishing, August 2, 2023, https://www.health.harvard.edu/blog/plyometrics-three-explosive-exercises-even-beginners-can-try-202308022960.

2. Lark Allen, "New Year's Resolutions Statistics and Trends," Drive Research, September 13, 2023, https://www.driveresearch.com/market-research-company-blog/new-years-resolutions-statistics/.

3. United States Census Bureau, "Census Bureau Estimates Show Average One-Way Travel Time to Work Rises to All-Time High," Census.gov, March 18, 2021, https://www.census.gov/newsroom/press-releases/2021/one-way-travel-time-to-work-rises.html.

4. Esteban Ortiz-Ospina, Charlie Giattino, and Max Roser, "Time Use," Our World in Data, November 2020, revised February 2024, https://ourworldindata.org/time-use.

5. U.S. Bureau of Labor Statistics, "American Time Use Survey Summary," June 22, 2023, https://www.bls.gov/news.release/atus.nr0.htm.

6. Ortiz-Ospina, Giattino, and Roser, "Time Use."

7. See: https://www.statista.com/statistics/256300/time-spent-with-media-worldwide/.

8. Michael Gross, "Shopping with Hunter Gatherers," *Current Biology* 32, no. 12 (June 2022): R596–R599, https://www.cell.com/current-biology/fulltext/S0960-9822(22)00905-8.

9. Bethany Turner-Livermore, PhD (Professor of Anthropology at Georgia State University) in discussion with the author on January 23, 2023. Subsequent quotations taken from the same interview.

10. Oxford Reference, s.v. "Helmuth von Moltke 1800–91 Prussian military commander," accessed July 17, 2024, https://www.oxfordreference.com/display/10.1093/acref/9780198826719.001.0001/q-oro-ed4-00007547.

Chapter 20

1. David Brooks, "The Art of Focus," *The New York Times*, June 2, 2014, https://www.nytimes.com/2014/06/03/opinion/brooks-the-art-of-focus.html.

2. Ecclesiastes 7:1. New Living Translation.

3. David Gibson, *Living Life Backward: How Ecclesiastes Teaches Us to Live in Light of the End* (Wheaton, IL: Crossway, 2017), 96.

About the Author

SHANE JACKSON leads Jackson Healthcare®, the parent company of more than twenty healthcare workforce businesses that serve over ten million patients each year. Championing its mission of improving the delivery of patient care and the lives of everyone it touches, he has led the organization through growth that has landed it on the *Forbes* list of America's Largest Private Companies; placement on the 100 Best Companies to Work For® and Best Workplaces in Health Care™ lists by *Fortune*; a spot on the Companies that Care list by PEOPLE®; and nearly a decade of Great Place To Work® certification.

The author of two books—*This Is the Thing: About Life, Joy, and Owning Your Purpose* (2025) and *Fostering Culture: A Leader's Guide to Purposefully Shaping Culture* (2018)—Shane also has written for *Fast Company* and *Forbes* on the topics of leadership, workplace culture, and living and leading with intention.

Shane serves on multiple boards, is co-founder of the leader-led goBeyondProfit business initiative, and has been named an Entrepreneur Of The Year® Southeast winner by Ernst & Young. In his spare time, he has competed in triathlon, acted in feature length films, and coached numerous youth sports teams, including at the highest levels of travel softball. He holds an MBA from Emory University and a business administration degree from Harding University. Married for a quarter century and counting, he and his wife are the proud parents of three. Learn more at shanejackson.com.